AMERICAN WILDFLOWER FLORILEGIUM

AMERICAN WILDFLOWER FLORILEGIUM

WRITTEN AND ILLUSTRATED BY
JEAN ANDREWS

Foreword
by
GHILLEAN T. PRANCE

Introduction
by
E. ARTHUR BELL

University of North Texas Press, Denton

PUBLICATION OF THIS BOOK WAS MADE POSSIBLE IN PART BY A GRANT FROM THE LEE AND ALBERT H. HALFF FUND OF COMMUNITIES FOUNDATION OF TEXAS.

Requests for permission to reproduce material from this book should be sent to:
Permissions
University of North Texas Press
Post Office Box 13856
Denton, TX 76203

Library of Congress Cataloging-in-Publication Data
Andrews, Jean
foreword by Ghillean T. Prance—1st ed.
introduction by E. Arthur Bell—1st ed.
p. cm.
Includes index

ISBN 0-929398-43-2

1. Wildflowers—North America.   2. Wildflowers—North America—Pictorial works.
3. Botanical Illustration—North America.
I. Title.
QK112.A43 1992
582.13′097—dc20 92–22135
CIP

DEDICATED TO

BILLIE LEE TURNER,

RECIPIENT OF THE

ASA GRAY AWARD OF THE AMERICAN SOCIETY OF PLANT TAXONOMISTS,

AND MY FRIEND.

CONTENTS

FLORILEGIUM AND BOTANICAL ART

By

GHILLEAN T. PRANCE

The term florilegium is derived from the Latin words *flos,* meaning flower, and *legere,* meaning to gather. The latter was specifically applied to a collection of flowers, but it was also used generally for a special selection of plants, paintings or poems. It has most often been applied to notable collections of flower paintings, especially of garden flowers. The earliest printed florilegium seems to be Adrian Collaert's *Florilegium,* published in Anver in Holland in 1593. Only a few copies of this rare work exist, one of which is in the Hunt Botanical Library in Pittsburgh. Florilegia were a development of the latter part of the sixteenth century because that was the period in which flowers were first cultivated extensively for their beauty rather than their utility.

Not all works that can be defined as florilegia bear this word in their titles. For example, two early florilegia which followed Collaert's were the beautiful *Le jardin de Roy tres Chrestien Henri IV* by Pierre Vallet, published in 1608, and *Hortus floridus* by Crispin Van de Passe, issued in 1614. Since that time, however, most beautiful works of botanical art have used the term florilegium.

Botanical art is a special form of art which combines scientific accuracy with artistic skill. Botanical artists usually have a special love for their subject and considerable knowledge of the structure and function of plants, which is certainly true of Jean Andrews, the author and the artist of this florilegium. Botanical art portrays enough detail of the plant so that it can be identified, but at the same time arranges it on the painting in such a way that it has aesthetic appeal. Botanical art is best defined by looking at the superb examples presented in this volume.

I am delighted to have the opportunity to define these two terms for Jean Andrews, who has done so much to draw attention to the spectacular flora of America.

Ghillean T. Prance, Director
Royal Botanic Gardens, Kew, England

INTRODUCTION

By

E. ARTHUR BELL

It is a privilege and a pleasure to introduce this delightful volume.

Dr. Andrews is a lady of remarkably wide interests and abilities. Her formal qualifications include a bachelor's degree in Home Economics, a master's degree in Art and Education and a doctorate in Art. Hiding behind all these qualifications is a talented field naturalist who is deeply interested in the plants and animals that she paints so superbly well. She is an authority on the world's peppers, and her beautifully illustrated book *Peppers: The Domesticated Capsicums* is a fascinating fund of information on the history, biology, agronomy and economic uses of these plants. It also demonstrates admirably the author's versatility, knowledge and scientific curiosity. Other publications of more regional interest which again highlight these qualities include *Sea Shells of the Texas Coast, Mollusca: A Biological Survey of the Padre Island National Seashore*, and *The Texas Bluebonnet*.

Her encouragement and support for both the arts and sciences have been extensive. She presently serves as a Trustee of the Laguna Gloria Art Museum in Austin, Texas, the National Wildflower Research Center and the Texas Botanical Garden Society. She is a member of the Advisory Council of the College of Natural Science, and the Visiting Committees to the Departments of Botany and Human Ecology in The University of Texas at Austin, and is a Friend of The University of Texas Brackenridge Field Laboratory. Most notably, however, she has endowed two positions within The University of Texas that bear her name: a Visiting Professorship in Human Nutrition, and a Visiting Professorship in Tropical and Economic Botany. Jean Andrews' contribution to the arts and sciences can be measured not only by her own achievements, but also by the achievements of those whom she has encouraged and helped.

Those of us who study plants make use of floras. These are descriptive catalogues, as nearly complete as the authors can make them, of all the plants that grow in a particular geographical region. A florilegium is not a flora but something much less regimented. A florilegium is literally a gathering of flowers, and in the *American Wildflower Florilegium* we find gathered the paintings of fifty-two flowering plants, native and introduced, and much information about them. The selection made by the author introduces or re-introduces to us some of the most beautiful of American wildflowers and the text provides concise information concerning nomenclature, classification, distribution, biology, propagation, uses and other aspects of interest. This book is a work of art, but it is also a valuable source of reference.

At the present time much attention is being given, and rightly so, to the destruction of the tropical rain forests. The loss of wildflowers in the temperate regions of the world may seem trivial in comparison, but these flowering plants are also part of an integrated ecosystem. Their disappearance not only diminishes the quality of our lives, but also threatens the lives of other animal and plant species that depend upon them.

While many of the species illustrated in the *Florilegium* are relatively common, human activity and changes of land use can rapidly reduce plant populations. We must be aware not only of the possible extinction of very rare species but also of the rapid decline in numbers of species that were once common. The beauty of many wildflowers, as seen through the eyes of this artist, would alone merit our efforts to preserve them. Flowering plants are more than objects of beauty, however. They are our very life support system, providing us directly or indirectly with the food that we eat and the oxygen that we breathe. They also provide us with fuel, fibres, dyes, paper, insecticides, drugs and countless other useful products. Of the many species known to be used in traditional medicine, nine are mentioned in the *Florilegium*. Few have been studied scientifically to determine whether their reputations are justified and, if so, what drugs they contain. It is a matter of great concern that so little is known about the chemical constituents and economical potential of most of the world's plants. It is pleasing that information on the uses of the chosen species has been included in this volume. This information emphasizes the many ways in which we depend on flowering plants and the urgent need to protect the plant kingdom and develop it for the benefit of mankind. We must all be grateful to Dr. Andrews for sharing with us the flowers that she has gathered.

E. Arthur Bell, C.B., Ph.D.
Former Director Royal Botanic Gardens, Kew, England
Adjunct Professor of Botany, The University of Texas at Austin
Visiting Professor, King's College, University of London

PREFACE TO THE PLATES

By

JEAN ANDREWS

Youth has its passions and I had mine—loves, children, family, wars, acquiring things, to name a few. However, aging has its own rewards—time to enjoy the fruits of those early passions and to build on wisdom gained; time to think, travel, savor your children's lives, enjoy your acquisitions; leisure to develop less demanding passions such as the study of oft-told or little-known tales of past happenings, distant places, and ancient people; finding your roots; sharing yourself and your possessions with others; seeing things you never had time to see—like wildflowers. One of the nicest things anyone ever said to me was about wildflowers. One day an old rancher friend offered me a bedraggled little bouquet of blossoms strangling in his rough-browned hand, then looked at me with eyes spent squinting in the Texas sun and said gruffly but softly, "I never saw the flowers until I knew you." Indeed, when I first knew him and his ranch, which was five hundred miles north of my own, I would point towards a strange wildflower and ask, "what is that?" His disgusted rejoinder would be, "that's a weed." Like peppers before them, wildflowers have brought me new joys and new friends. For my son and his wife's Christmas present one year I planted their lakeside meadow with wildflowers so that during the winter Robin and Ann might happily anticipate the promise of bloom, in the spring enjoy the colorful flowers, during summer gather seed, and sow come fall with the hope that the annual blooms would remind them of our times together.

Beginning with the bluebonnet, each flower I discovered led to another until the urge to share my new love with others by painting them led me to this book. But what could I do to my paintings so that they would not be just duplications, and how could they be both aesthetically pleasing and scientifically correct while making a contribution to botany? To that end I have attempted to do things a camera cannot do by making my paintings composites through time which present, when size permits, several views of the blossom along with the buds, seed pods, fruits, roots, and at least one leaf in detail in such a manner that the growth pattern of the plant is discernable. In nature, blooms and seed or fruit may not occur at the same time on the same plant.

Before I began painting for this *American Wildflower Florilegium*, I decided to make a list containing fifty wildflowers. Dr. David Northington, director of the National Wildflower Research Center, helped with the selection. Our initial list containing fifty-two species to be illustrated was entirely unscientific and reflected to a great extent our personal preferences, although we tried to get a balance with representatives of the major plant groups from wide-spread locations in the United States. Availability and travel time are but two of the factors that led me to make changes in the initial list. This now seems like an offhand way to put a book together, but it was often impossible to find a particular plant, hence the name *florilegium* (flo-rili-dzium), a gathering of flowers. Many of them may be old favorites of yours as they were mine.

It is appropriate that I am writing the preface to these plates of American wildflowers as I spend a glorious June in bloom-filled Great Britain. The British contributions to botany and botanical art have been many and great. The Royal Botanic Gardens at Kew have set the pattern and standards for botanical exploration, study, preservation, art, and display for the rest of the world. Botanists from the British Isles were responsible for discovering, naming, or describing the largest part of the species in this book.

As I drive through the British countryside I am thrilled to see fields of the scarlet corn poppies, blue corn flowers, and snowy ox-eye daisies that you will find in this book. Today they also grace American highways as a result of introduction by our British ancestors nearly four centuries ago. Those Old World wildflower seeds came to the New World with the equally foreign "corn" to feed the colonists and their livestock. In the English language corn was the generic name for all bread grains before Columbus discovered American maize. Poppies and corn flowers grew in the grain fields, hence the flowers of the "corn" fields became corn flowers and corn poppies, while maize became Indian corn, later just corn. As a salute to those contributions I have invited past and present directors of the Kew Gardens to help me explain what I've attempted to do.

For five years my car was never without the where-with-all to collect a plant. I'd be sailing down a Texas highway when I'd spot a big clump of some elusive wildflower, slam on the brakes, pull off the road, and jump out to record it on film before collecting it for the drawing table. Let me caution! Before lying on your stomach to get that perfect angle, look at the ground very carefully. Although you think you might lose your mind as you are suddenly blanketed with a stinging horde of fire ants running faster than you can swat, they may be one of the lesser evils you might lie down in. I am no longer surprised where one might find a delicate bloom. Wildflowers are very plebeian, often any old rubbish pile, crack in the pavement, or yard of a deserted shack will do.

Not counting the preliminaries, I spent a minimum of forty hours actual drawing/painting time—usually more—on each painting. Painting time was lonely time because the flowers would not wait for me to visit on the telephone or lunch with friends; I had to work straight through their brief life spans. To reduce the tedium I listened to books-on-tape. Biographies and history are my favorites, so I kept company with the great.

I have packed up my painting gear to go work in a small-town motel room near a swamp full of insect-eating plants, or commandeered the dining table of a friend for days when I worked to paint a distant bloom. Shy trilliums beckoned me to Oregon. In my haste, I left my special paper on the plane. Its replacement cost me most of a day.

Painting flowers, or anything, from nature is a matter of working against the clock. In every moment that passes, something changes. Buds open, petals fall, stems change position, leaves curl, and colors fade. You are in a stressful race against the time when the flower will die and collapse. This pressure builds even more when there is not another specimen available. Since I only work from living plant material, I have had to learn ways to trick the flower into lasting a few moments more. At times I've sensed what Paul Cezanne must have felt when he broke down and cried because the apples in his still-life arrangement withered and spoiled before he had finished the painting. The Missouri Evening Primrose, a night bloomer, was my most trying subject. I had luck tricking other flowers with limited opening time to remain open, but none of my subterfuges prevailed with this one. One blistering June I rose before daylight and drove fifty miles a day for a week in order to study the big yellow blossom *in situ*, as it stubbornly refused to remain open if disturbed on its forbidding caliche bank.

Since my paintings are composites through time, I have often painted up to the attachment site and then waited weeks—even until the next year—for the next stage of growth in order to place a bud, a seed pod, or a fruit in its proper place. Each species has been drawn in the same scale to the others as they are in nature so that when they are reduced in the same proportion they continue to relate to one another as they do in the wild. Limited paper size forced me to devise a convention—two separated lines—which would indicate that the height of the plant was beyond those limits. I hope this does not prove to be too obtrusive, but I find identification is very confusing when short plants are shown the same size as tall plants just so they can be made to fit on a page.

I work on a smooth Strathmore 3-ply paper which I purchase all at one time so that it will be consistent. The paint is opaque watercolor, preferably casein, but that is not often found today so I substitute gouache. Underpaintings of these colors are overlaid with prisma-colors and pencil. After years of doing these paintings I no longer make preliminary drawings. Instead I make photocopies of the plant and bloom when enough are available, then make my measurements from those images so that the plant doesn't get worn out from handling. During the painting the plant is growing in a pot or is in water in a small narrow container or floral tubes. The color work is done in daylight. Light is one of the reasons I do not color all the foliage—that way I can work with artificial light at night and not make mistakes with the color. Greens are so variable.

No matter the precautions, it is extremely difficult to keep the background perfectly clean. Some of the paintings were seven years old when the book went to press. Everything changes with age. Strange yellow spots appeared on the California Poppy three years after it was painted. In an effort to keep soil and the Texas cockroaches at bay, the paintings were kept in plastic sleeves. Perhaps there was a reaction with paper, paint, or my body oils to the acetate, who knows? The spotting could have been eliminated mechanically but I did not want the background dropped out.

Many friends, especially botany doctoral student Katy McKinney and xeriscape specialist Waldi Browning, became spotters who located plants for me, while the NWRC horticulturist, Eleanor Crank, grew several hard-to-find species. Once I had completed the paintings, the initial identifications were verified by Dr. Marshall C. Johnson, co-author of *Manual of the Vascular Plants of Texas*. At the NWRC, botanist Beth Anderson, with research director Dr. John Avrett, made the initial survey of the literature using a form I had designed. This form evolved from a prototype I had used in collecting information for my shell books. It worked so well that it was incorporated into those books and was happily received by harried researchers who found it simplified the search for particular information without the need to read the entire description. For example, if the reader only wants to know how the flower is pollinated, or how to propagate it, there is no need to look at other categories. The descriptions and the plates are arranged in alphabetical order by scientific name.

At The University of Texas at Austin, taxonomist Dr. Guy Newsom helped me search for references of each species. Dr. Jack Neff, pollination expert, checked pollinators. When the forms were completed to the best of my amateur-botanist ability, taxonomist Professor Billie Lee Turner checked them. Turner over-extended himself to make certain all the information was not only taxonomically and scientifically correct but also as up-to-date as possible. No one could have had a scientific advisor more devoted to excellence.

I could name others who helped me, including the entire faculty of the Department of Botany at The University of Texas at Austin, whose acceptance of me and my work has not only been reassuring but also very complimentary. I am forever indebted to all who have helped me in this endeavor. Thank you!

For those busy folks who love our American wildflowers but would like the pain taken out of learning more about them, I humbly give you this *American Wildflower Floriliegum*—my gathering of flowers. Enjoy!

PLATES

This Book was drawn
by
Jean Andrews
(from the Life growing)
between the years 1985 and 1990

GOLDEN COLUMBINE

SCIENTIFIC NAME:
Aquilegia chrysantha Gray 1873

FAMILY:
RANUNCULACEAE

LIFE HISTORY:
Biennial herb.

ORIGIN:
Southwestern United States.

RANGE:
From Texas to Arizona, New Mexico, Colorado and south to Mexico.

DESCRIPTION:
PLANT: Erect, to nearly 3′ tall. Compound leaves divided into 2 or 3 leaflets.
FLOWER: Flowers yellow, 2″–3″ long. Sepals are yellow, resembling petals. Long spurs on each of the 5 petals.

BLOOM PERIOD:
July to August

POLLINATOR(S):
Hummingbirds? perhaps moths?

HABITAT REQUIREMENTS:
Found on moist, well-drained slopes, near streams, and rocky ravines at higher altitudes. Partial shade.

PROPAGATION:
Sow seeds in spring in well-drained slightly acidic soil. Columbines are difficult to move once they are established. Excellent addition to rock gardens.

REMARKS & ETYMOLOGY:
The genus name is from the Latin *Aquilegia* meaning eagle, referring to the shape of the claw-like petals or spurs. The species name *chrysantha* describes the golden color of the flowers. Asa Gray, "The Father of American Botany" first described this species. Professor E. B. Payson (1893–1927), botanist at the University of Wyoming, rendered an excellent account of the genus (cited below).

Although the long spurs with nectar cups in the tips were designed for hummingbirds, bees often reach the nectar by punching holes in the top of the spur through which they sip the sweet liquid.

SPECIES IN AMERICA:
About 100 species mostly in temperate montane regions.

REFERENCES:

Gray, A.
1873   *Proc. Amer. Acad. Arts* 8:621.
Munz, P. A.
1946   The cultivated and wild Columbines. *Gentes Herb.* 7:138–39.
Payson, E. B.
1918   The North American species of *Aquilegia. Contr. U.S. Natl. Herb.* 20:133–58.

WHITE PRICKLY POPPY

SCIENTIFIC NAME:
Argemone albiflora Hornemann 1815

FAMILY:
PAPAVERACEAE

LIFE HISTORY:
Annual or biennial herb.

ORIGIN:
Mexico.

RANGE:
From northern Arkansas to Missouri and Texas.

DESCRIPTION:
PLANT: Erect, 3'–4' tall, with prickly stems and leaves. When cut, yellow latex oozes from stems.
FLOWER: Flowers solitary or in clusters. White petals with numerous yellow or reddish stamens, 4″ in diameter.

BLOOM PERIOD:
March to June.

POLLINATOR(S):
Pollen-collecting bees, small insects, especially pollen-feeding scarab beetles.

HABITAT REQUIREMENTS:
Sandy or gravelly soils in disturbed areas, roadsides, pastures and fence rows. Full sun.

PROPAGATION:
Seeds form in hard, prickly pods. Collect when dry. Wear gloves and use clippers. There is no information on propagation but the species is known to have been cultivated for a long time.

REMARKS & ETYMOLOGY:
A Danish botanist, J. W. Hornemann, (1770–1841) described this spiny plant, giving it the name *albiflora*, (*alba* = white) after its showy bloom. *Argemone* is the name of a similar herbaceous plant mentioned by Pliny.

All parts of the plant are somewhat poisonous. Its prickly foliage protects it from livestock and other animals, which allows for fields of showy, white blooms. It is a good indicator of lands that have been overgrazed. It is often considered a noxious weed even though it was introduced and cultivated in European gardens before 1812. The entire plant can be used for dyes and the seed for oil, which is burned in lamps, and is also used as a laxative in Mexico. Blooms are often covered with beetles and their droppings.

SPECIES IN AMERICA:
About 30 species in North and South America.

REFERENCES:

Hornemann, J. W.
   1815   *Hort. Haft.* 489.
Ownbey, G. B.
   1958   Monograph of the genus *Argemone* for North America and the West Indies. *Mem. Torrey Bot. Club* 21:1–159.
   1961   The genus *Argemone* in South America and Hawaii. *Brittonia* 13: 9–109.

BROADLEAF ASTER
TEXAS ASTER

SCIENTIFIC NAME:
Aster drummondii ssp. *texanus*
(Burgess) 1906, Jones 1984

FAMILY:
ASTERACEAE (= COMPOSITAE)

LIFE HISTORY:
Perennial herb.

ORIGIN:
North America.

RANGE:
From Louisiana to Arkansas to the eastern half of Texas.

DESCRIPTION:
PLANT: Erect, 1′–3′ tall. Ovate leaves 1″–5″ long.
FLOWER: Bluish-white or lavender ray flowers surrounding yellow disk flowers. Flower heads ½″–¾″ diameter, in terminal clusters.

BLOOM PERIOD:
August to November.

POLLINATOR(S):
Butterflies, bees, other insects.

HABITAT REQUIREMENTS:
Prefers loam or well-drained clay soils of open woods and prairies. Full sun to partial or dappled shade.

PROPAGATION:
Collect seed in late fall or early winter, as soon as it matures. Root divisions can be made in late fall or early spring. Asters can become rather aggressive in gardens.

REMARKS & ETYMOLOGY:
The genus name, *aster,* which means star in Greek, refers to the plant's star-like blossoms. One Greek legend associates asters with the god Virgo, who looked down from heaven and wept. His star dust tears became asters. Ancient Greeks believed that asters were sacred to the gods and goddesses. The species name honors Thomas Drummond (1780–1835), a Scottish botanist, who collected plants in Texas in the 1830s. Several subspecies are recognized for this widespread variable species, as noted by Almut G. Jones (1923–), a native of Germany, botanist at the University of Illinois at Urbana–Champaign, who refers the material drawn here to the subspecies *texanus.*

An unforgettable sight in my garden one fall day was a blossom-covered Texas Aster plant blanketed with Monarch butterflies resting and refueling during their annual migration to Mexico. The brilliant orange and black winged insects lingered amid the lavender flowers for three days before continuing their mysterious southward journey.

SPECIES IN AMERICA:
About 250 species found in temperate zones.

REFERENCES:

Burgess, E. S.
  1903   In *Flora of the southeastern United States.* Edited by J. K. Small, 1214, 1339.
  1906   Species and variations of biotian asters, with discussion of variability in *Aster. Mem. Torrey Bot. Club* 13:1–419.
Jones, A. G.
  1984   Nomenclatural notes on *Aster* (Asteraceae) II. *Phytologia.* 55:380–88.

WINECUP
POPPY MALLOW

SCIENTIFIC NAME:
Callirhoe involucrata Torrey & Gray 1849

FAMILY:
MALVACEAE

LIFE HISTORY:
Perennial herb.

ORIGIN:
United States.

RANGE:
From North Dakota to Wyoming and Utah, south to Missouri, Oklahoma and Texas.

DESCRIPTION:
PLANT: Sprawling, 6″–12″ tall, with long trailing stems. Leaves deeply incised into 5–7 lobes.
FLOWER: Goblet-shaped burgundy flowers, petals to 2″ in length. Three bract-like structures beneath the sepals are collectively called the involucre.

BLOOM PERIOD:
February to June.

POLLINATOR(S):
Solitary bees, including *Diadasia afflicta*, a specialist which restricts its pollen collection to *Callirhoe* flowers.

HABITAT REQUIREMENTS:
Sandy or gravelly soils of open woods, rocky hills and thickets. Full sun.

PROPAGATION:
Seed is not available commercially, but hand-collected seed can be sown in the fall. Needs well-drained soil. Tuber can also be divided and replanted in fall or winter.

REMARKS & ETYMOLOGY:
In Greek mythology Kallo was the beautiful daughter of Achelous. The species name refers to the involucre around each flower as noted in the above. Asa Gray (1810–1888) was a prominent botanist at Harvard, and John Torrey (1796–1873) was a botanist from New York.

Although winecups cannot be found in most nurseries, they have potential as bedding plants or hanging baskets. The roots of an European relative of the winecup exude a sticky sap which is used in making marshmallows. The pleasant-tasting roots were eaten by native Americans.

SPECIES IN AMERICA:
About 7 species in the southeastern regions of the United States and closely adjacent Mexico.

REFERENCES:

Dorr, L. T.
    1983   The systematics and evolution of the genus *Callirhoe* (Malvaceae). Unpublished dissertation D7374, Univ. Texas at Austin.
Torrey, J. & A. Gray
    1849   *Plantae Fendlerianae Novi-Mexicanae* 16.

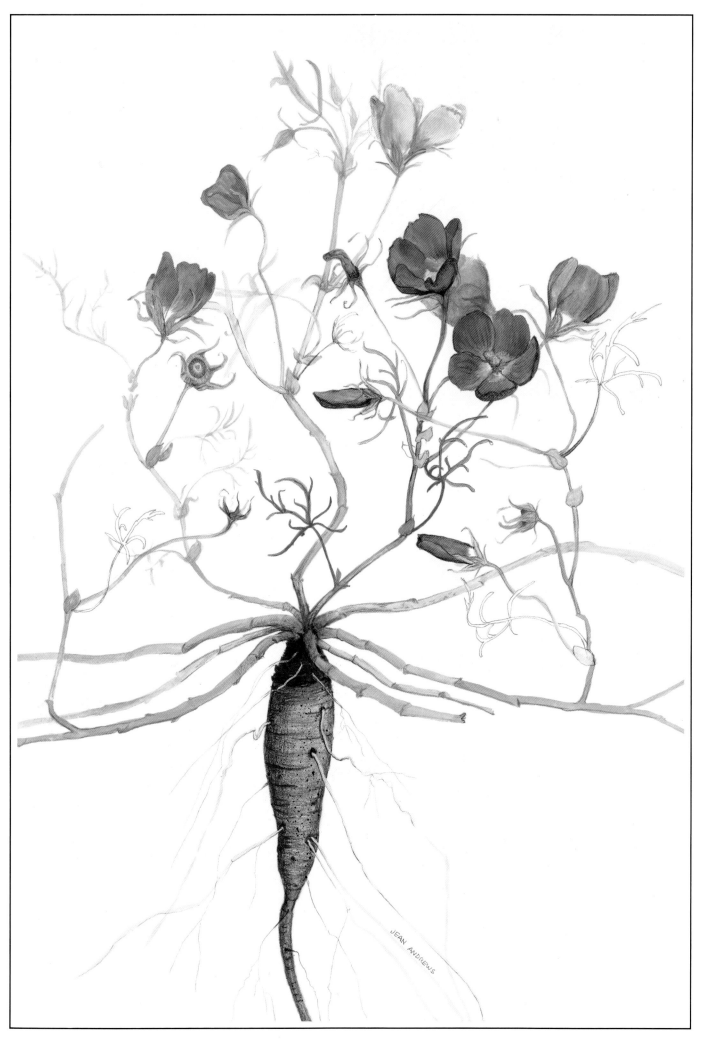

SQUARE BUD PRIMROSE

SCIENTIFIC NAME:
Calylophus berlandieri Spach 1835

FAMILY:
ONAGRACEAE

LIFE HISTORY:
Annual or weak perennial herb.

ORIGIN:
North America.

RANGE:
From southeastern Kansas to southeastern Colorado, eastern New Mexico, western Oklahoma and west and south Texas.

DESCRIPTION:
PLANT: Upright, bush, semi-woody, 6″–24″ tall. Narrow leaves 1″–3″ long.
FLOWER: Yellow flowers, about 2″ diameter, with a black or yellow stigma and throat (may be a combination of those colors).

BLOOM PERIOD:
March to November.

POLLINATOR(S):
A wide array of insects, most importantly the robust beetle.

HABITAT REQUIREMENTS:
Dry, sandy soils of prairies and open areas. Full sun.

PROPAGATION:
Collect seed and sow in the fall.

REMARKS & ETYMOLOGY:
Calylophus was named for Calliope, a Greek muse with a beautiful voice. Edouard Spach (1801–1879), a French botanist, described this plant, which he named in honor of Jean Louis Berlandier (1805–1851), a Franco-Swiss botanical explorer. Berlandier collected plants and kept a journal of his activities during an expedition into Mexico (which included Texas) in 1828.

The flowers open at dawn and last but one day. The highly contrasting, blackish-red spot on the clear yellow bloom of some varieties may be designed to attract the pollinator. Their compact shapes and heat tolerance make them good rock garden plants.

SPECIES IN AMERICA:
About five species in Texas and Mexico.

REFERENCES:

Spach, E.
    1835   *Ann. Sci. Nat. Bot.* Ser. 2, 4:272.
Towner, H. F.
    1977   Biosystematics of *Calylophus* (Onagraceae). *Ann. Missouri Bot. Gard.* 64:48–120.

TRUMPET CREEPER
TRUMPET HONEYSUCKLE
COW ITCH

SCIENTIFIC NAME:
Campsis radicans Seemann 1867

FAMILY:
BIGNONIACEAE

LIFE HISTORY:
Perennial, deciduous, woody climber.

ORIGIN:
North America.

RANGE:
From New Jersey to Ohio and Iowa, south to Florida and Texas.

DESCRIPTION:
PLANT: Woody vine to over 30′, climbs by aerial rootlets. Compound, deciduous, opposite leaves with 9 to 11 leaflets.
FLOWER: Trumpet-shaped, reddish-orange flowers with waxy petals. Arranged in terminal panicles, the flowers are 2″–3″ in length; the calyx is the same color as the corolla.

BLOOM PERIOD:
May to September.

POLLINATOR(S):
Hummingbirds and large bees (*Bombus*).

HABITAT REQUIREMENTS:
Found climbing on trees in moist woods, along fence rows, and in old fields. Adapted to various soil types. Full to part sun.

PROPAGATION:
Winged seed capsules can be gathered after they have turned brown, but before they split open. Sow seeds in the fall immediately after collecting. Allow feathery seed to dry before storing. Seeds must be stratified (alternate freezing and thawing to help crack the seed coat) in order to germinate. Stem or root cuttings can also be taken.

REMARKS & ETYMOLOGY:
The graceful, curved stamens give rise to the genus name *Campsis* from the Greek *campsis*, something curved or bent. The species name, *radicans*, "with rooting stems," refers to the easily rooted stems. Berthold Carl Seemann (1825–1871) from Germany was the botanist on the voyage of the HMS *Herald*. He described numerous new species from along the west coast of North America.

Highly valued as an ornamental, this vine grows aggressively with little maintenance, providing good cover for chainlink fences and walls. Trumpet creeper is host to several genera of ants. The relationship is not requisite; however, certain protection may be offered by the ants in return for the plant's nectar. This partnership made painting this flower quite hazardous.

SPECIES IN AMERICA:
Only one species in North America; an additional species in Asia.

REFERENCES:

Bertin, R. I.
    1982   Paternity and fruit production in trumpet creeper. *Amer. Naturalist* 119:694–709.
Elias, T. S. & H. Gelband
    1975   Nectar: its production and functions in trumpet creeper. *Science* 189:289–90.
Seemann, B. C.
    1867   *J. Botany* 5:372.

INDIAN PAINTBRUSH
TEXAS PAINTBRUSH

SCIENTIFIC NAME:
Castilleja indivisa Engelmann 1845

FAMILY:
SCROPHULARIACEAE

LIFE HISTORY:
Annual herb.

ORIGIN:
North America.

RANGE:
Coastal Plain and eastern Texas, and southeastern Oklahoma.

DESCRIPTION:
PLANT: 6″–18″ tall; grows in clumps; pubescent stems and leaves.
FLOWER: What appear at first glance to be vermillion red "petals" are actually modified leaves called bracts. The small, 1″, somewhat inconspicuous, slender flowers found in axils of the bracts are creamy, pinkish-yellow or yellow-green. There is considerable variation in the shades of red among the various species of Castilleja.

BLOOM PERIOD:
March to May.

POLLINATOR(S):
Butterflies, hummingbirds.

HABITAT REQUIREMENTS:
Prefers well-drained sandy loam soils; also found in calcareous soils of road sides is C. purpurea and yet other species. Full sun.

PROPAGATION:
Seed in open, sunny sites for best results. It is yet to be determined if seeds require a cold, wet treatment for a period of time in order to germinate. The seeds are exceptionally small, with millions per pound. Seeding rate is ¼ pound per acre. Research indicates that seedlings grow more vigorously in the presence of a host species. Semiparasitic in nature, Castilleja draws water and nutrients from the roots of plants to which they attach. Seeds are formed in dehiscent capsules as the flowers age. Capsules may be collected carefully by hand when they become brown and dry. Seeds are very expensive.

REMARKS & ETYMOLOGY:
Indian paintbrush was first described by George Engelmann (1809–1884), a German-born American botanist. The genus name honors Domingo Castillejo, an early Spanish botanist. The narrow leaves are usually undivided, hence the name indivisa.

The genus Castilleja occurs from the southern Andes of South America northwards through Central America and Mexico to Alaska. In Texas there is a rather long legend concerning Indians, bluebonnets and a paintbrush. Briefly, an old Indian chief used this paintbrush and red earth to paint some of the blue flowers red when ordered to do so by the Great Spirit. An enemy appeared among the blue flowers. A group of strange warriors with red faces (as many as the flowers the chief had painted) took up spears and drove the enemy away. Among the red flowers was found the old Indian's paintbrush. Even today, you see Indian Paintbrush and Bluebonnets growing together.

SPECIES IN AMERICA:
Over 150 species in western North America, Mexico and Central America.

REFERENCES:

Engelmann, G., A. Gray & J. W. Blakenship
1845   Pl. Lindheimeriana 1:47.
Holmgren, N. H.
1970   Castilleja. In Manual of the Vascular Plants of Texas, edited by D. S. Correll and M. C. Johnston, 1439–42.

BASKET FLOWER
STAR THISTLE

SCIENTIFIC NAME:
Centaurea americana Nuttall 1821

FAMILY:
ASTERACEAE (= COMPOSITAE)

LIFE HISTORY:
Annual herb.

ORIGIN:
North America.

RANGE:
From Missouri to Arizona, south to Louisiana, Texas and Mexico.

DESCRIPTION:
PLANT: Thick, sparsely-branched stems, 2'–5' tall. Leaves are sessile (attached directly to stem without a petiole).
FLOWER: Flower heads borne singly on stem. Bisexual, pink (outer) and cream (inner) disk flowers. No ray flowers.

BLOOM PERIOD:
Late spring to summer.

POLLINATOR(S):
Bees, butterflies.

HABITAT REQUIREMENTS:
Sandy or clayey loams of roadsides, disturbed areas and prairies. Full sun.

PROPAGATION:
Seed is not widely available commercially, but can be easily collected by picking the rather large, black seeds from the dry heads. Plant seed in the early fall.

REMARKS & ETYMOLOGY:
The genus name comes from the Greek word *kentaur* for centaur, a mythical beast, half man/half horse, who was thought to use this plant medicinally. The common name refers to the intricate, woven structure beneath the flower head. Thomas Nuttall (1786–1859), a British Naturalist and an early botanical explorer of the United States, first described the species.

Although a member of the thistle tribe and often confused with the thistle, basket flower does not have spines. The dried flowers make nice additions to dried floral arrangements, while the tall plant is beautiful against a garden wall.

SPECIES IN AMERICA:
Although there are between 300 and 400 herbaceous species native to Eurasia, only this one is indigenous to North America.

REFERENCES:

Greenman, J. M.
    1904   Notes on Southwestern and Mexican Plants: Indigenous *Centaureas* of North America. *Bot. Gaz.* 37:220–21.
Nuttall, T.
    1821   *J. Acad. Nat. Sci. Phil.* 2:117.

BACHELOR'S BUTTON
CORN FLOWER

SCIENTIFIC NAME:
Centaurea cyanus Linnaeus 1753

FAMILY:
ASTERACEAE (= COMPOSITAE)

LIFE HISTORY:
Annual herb.

ORIGIN:
Southeastern Europe and Sicily.

RANGE:
Widely cultivated and frequently escaping. Naturalized throughout the eastern United States and other regions.

DESCRIPTION:
PLANT: Slender, erect, mostly 1'–3' tall. Leaves grayish with cottony hairs.
FLOWER: Blue, bisexual, flower heads, occasionally purple, white, or pink, about 1½" in diameter.

BLOOM PERIOD:
Spring to summer.

POLLINATOR(S):
Bees.

HABITAT REQUIREMENTS:
Found in disturbed areas along roadsides and in fields. Full sun.

PROPAGATION:
Seed commercially available. Often component of wild flower mixes. Sow in spring or fall. It self-sows readily.

REMARKS & ETYMOLOGY:
Named by the father of modern botany, Carolus Linnaeus (1707–1778), the generic name refers to the Greek mythology in which centaurs used the plant for medicinal purposes. *Cyanus* describes the blue color. The flower heads have been likened to certain ragged-cloth buttons once worn by gentlemen, hence the name Bachelor's Button.

Members of the genus are related to thistles but lack the spines. Though considered a cosmopolitan weed, corn flowers have long been a garden favorite. Corn flowers were inadvertently introduced to America by the early colonists of Virginia, along with other field flowers such as the poppy and ox-eye daisy when hay was shipped from Europe to feed their livestock. Today the traveler can see fields of Bachelor's Buttons in Virginia and other eastern seaboard states from which they are spreading.

SPECIES IN AMERICA:
Primarily an Old World genus of numerous species, many of these introduced in North America, have become abundant, often noxious weeds along roadsides and in fields.

REFERENCES:

Greenman, J. M.
    1904   Notes on Southwestern & Mexican Plants. *Bot. Gaz.* 37:219–22.
Linnaeus, C.
    1753   *Species Plantarum* 2:911.
Shinners, L. H.
    1951   Notes on Texas Compositae. *Field & Lab.* 19:136.

OX-EYE DAISY

SCIENTIFIC NAME:
Chrysanthemum leucanthemum Linnaeus 1753

FAMILY:
ASTERACEAE (= COMPOSITAE)

LIFE HISTORY:
Perennial herb.

ORIGIN:
China, Asia, Europe.

RANGE:
Naturalized from Europe; now found throughout eastern United States.

DESCRIPTION:
PLANT: Erect, to 3' tall. Leaves deeply toothed.
FLOWER: Flower heads 1"–2" diameter. White, female ray flowers surround bisexual, yellow disk flowers.

BLOOM PERIOD:
May to October.

POLLINATOR(S):
Butterflies, bees.

HABITAT REQUIREMENTS:
Found on various soils in meadows, waste areas and along roadsides. Full sun to partial shade.

PROPAGATION:
Seed can be sown in spring after danger of frost, and can be grown by division. Ox-eye daisy has been widely cultivated and bred in Europe.

REMARKS & ETYMOLOGY:
Ever since Carolus Linnaeus named this plant many botanical workers, including the French evolutionist Jean Baptiste Antoine Pierre Monnet de Lamarck (1744–1829), would place the species in the genus *Leucanthemum*. Such a move would cause the genus name and the species name to be the same, and such tautonyms are prevented by the International Code of Botanical Nomenclature. Interestingly, the code governing zoological nomenclature has no such restriction which results in our closest cousin, the chimpanzee, being *Pan pan*.

This plant originated in China, from whence it covered the globe. The ancient Chinese used this humble, white flower to begin the development of the many varieties of chrysanthemums which we enjoy today. Daisies have long been the object of many superstitions and rituals. The common name, daisy, is an alteration of "day's eye." It is difficult to imagine that our countryside was without the bright daisy before the European colonists brought it along in their hay.

SPECIES IN AMERICA:
100–200 species in the Northern Hemisphere, mainly in Europe and Asia.

REFERENCES:

Lamarck, J. B. A. P. M.
    1779   *Flore Française* 2:137.
Linnaeus, C.
    1753   *Species Plantarum* 888.
McVaugh, R.
    1984   *Chrysanthemum*. In *Flora Novo-Galiciana* 12:228–29.

CHICORY
BLUE SAILORS

SCIENTIFIC NAME:
Cichorium intybus Linnaeus 1735

FAMILY:
ASTERACEAE (= COMPOSITAE)

LIFE HISTORY:
Perennial herb.

ORIGIN:
Europe, Northern Africa, Western Asia.

RANGE:
Naturalized from Europe throughout most of United States and Canada.

DESCRIPTION:
PLANT: Upright to sprawling, to 4' tall. Large deep-growing taproot.
FLOWER: Flower heads 2" diameter. Light blue ray flowers; no disk flowers.

BLOOM PERIOD:
June to October.

POLLINATOR(S):
Bees.

HABITAT REQUIREMENTS:
Various soils in disturbed areas, fields and roadsides. Full sun.

PROPAGATION:
Plant seeds in either spring or fall. Seed is available commercially, and is often found in wildflower mixes. Tolerates infertile soils and is fairly drought tolerant.

REMARKS & ETYMOLOGY:
Cichorium is a variation of the Arabic name for the plant. The species name, *intybus,* comes from the Latin word for endive.

Chicory leaves can be eaten like endive. In Europe it is grown as a vegetable and as fodder for livestock. The large root has been roasted and ground to make a coffee substitute. This "coffee" is a diuretic and tonic, and was used to treat liver and gall bladder problems. Caffine-free chicory is a popular coffee additive in Louisiana. Brought to America by early European colonists, the plant can now be found growing in every corner and roadside of America, even from cracks in the pavement of our "urban jungles."

SPECIES IN AMERICA:
A single species introduced from the Old World.

REFERENCES:

Cichan, M. A. & B. F. Palser
    1982   Development of normal and seedless achenes in *Cichorium intybus* (Compositae). *Amer. J. Bot.* 69:885–95.
Kains, M. G.
    1937   Chicory. In *The Standard Cyclopedia of Horticulture.* Edited by L. H. Bailey. 747. New York: Macmillan Co.
Linnaeus, C.
    1753   *Species Plantarum* 813.

TEXAS THISTLE

SCIENTIFIC NAME:
Cirsium texanum Buckley 1862

FAMILY:
ASTERACEAE (= COMPOSITAE)

LIFE HISTORY:
Biennial or weak perennial herb.

ORIGIN:
North America.

RANGE:
From Oklahoma to Texas and Mexico.

DESCRIPTION:
PLANT: Upright, prickly plant, 2′–5′ tall. Leaves pinnately divided, and covered with dense, woolly hairs on the underside.
FLOWER: Pink or purplish, bisexual disk flowers (no ray flowers) with spiny bracts. Flower head up to 2″ diameter.

BLOOM PERIOD:
April to July.

POLLINATOR(S):
Butterflies, bees, and other insects.

HABITAT REQUIREMENTS:
Found in dry sand or clay soils of fields, roadsides and disturbed areas. Full sun.

PROPAGATION:
Not propagated, usually considered undesirable. However, seeds are easy to collect and plant in the fall.

REMARKS & ETYMOLOGY:
Cirsium, a word used by Dioscorides, is from *cirsos*, meaning a swollen vein, for which thistles were reputed to be a remedy. Samuel Botsford Buckley (1809–1884), an American naturalist, described this species.

Despite their spiny characteristics, thistles can be used in salads or as a vegetable. Leaves (once the spines are removed) and roots can be eaten raw. The cooked root tastes somewhat like the kindred artichoke. The seeds provide food for goldfinches and fluffy nest-lining materials for other birds. At times, on close inspection, many tiny ants may be found impaled on the spines of the involucral bracts.

SPECIES IN AMERICA:
About 150 species in north temperate regions.

REFERENCES:

Buckley, S. B.
    1862   *Proc. Acad. Nat. Sci. Philadelphia.* '1861'(1862) 400.
Howell, J. T.
    1957   Distribution data on weedy thistles in western North America. *Leafl. W. Bot.* 9:17–29.
Petrak, F.
    1917   Die nordamerikanischen Arten der Gattung *Cirsium. Beih. Bot. Centralbl.* 35, Abt. 2:223–567.

JEAN ANDREWS

DAY FLOWER

SCIENTIFIC NAME:
Commelina erecta Linnaeus 1753

FAMILY:
COMMELINACEAE

LIFE HISTORY:
Perennial herb.

ORIGIN:
Eastern and Southern United States.

RANGE:
From Wisconsin to Wyoming, and south to Florida and Arizona.

DESCRIPTION:
PLANT: Upright or sprawling, reaching height of 2′ or more. Leaves mostly in a cluster at the base.
FLOWER: Blue flowers, 1″ or more in diameter.

BLOOM PERIOD:
May to October.

POLLINATOR(S):
Pollen-collecting bees, since flowers lack nectar.

HABITAT REQUIREMENTS:
Grows in sandy or rocky soils of woodlands, fields, slopes and streambanks. Shade to partial sun.

PROPAGATION:
Not widely available from commercial sources, but seed can be collected and sown.

REMARKS & ETYMOLOGY:
The genus *Commelina* honors the three Dutch Commelin brothers, the three-petal flowers reflecting each brothers' life. The two prominent petals represent the two scholarly brothers, Johan (1629–1692) and Caspar (1667–1731), who published several botanical works. The stunted petal resembles a third brother, who made no contributions to botany. The specific name *erecta* refers to its erect habit.

The blossoms of dayflowers only last one day. The "widow's tears" appear when you gently squeeze the spathe which enclosed the flowers. The Day Flower adds a hard-to-find blue to a flower bed, but in the southwestern U.S.A. its smaller, less vibrant, look-alike, False Day Flower (*Commelinantia anomala*), will take over a garden, if allowed.

SPECIES IN AMERICA:
About 225 species in tropical and subtropical regions.

REFERENCES:

Linnaeus, C.
  1753   *Species Plantarum* 41.
Matuda, E.
  1955   Las Commenlinaceas Mexicanas. *An. Inst. Biol. Mex.* 26:333–34.

RAIN LILY
GIANT PRAIRIE LILY

SCIENTIFIC NAME:
Cooperia pedunculata Herbert 1936

FAMILY:
AMARYLLIDACEAE

LIFE HISTORY:
Perennial bulbous herb.

ORIGIN:
North America.

RANGE:
East, Central and South Texas, and Mexico.

DESCRIPTION:
PLANT: Small lily-like; grass-like leaves 6″–12″. Grows from large, tunicate bulb.
FLOWER: Trumpet-shaped flowers 2″–3″ in diameter, with three white or rose-tinged sepals and petals.

BLOOM PERIOD:
Intermittently from spring to fall.

POLLINATOR(S):
Hawk moths

HABITAT REQUIREMENTS:
Found in rich soils of open meadows and fields.

PROPAGATION:
Not available commercially. Bulbs can be transplanted from areas destined to be developed or from private lands, with the owner's permission. Seed are easily collected, but they drop quickly after maturity; the plants reseed readily.

REMARKS & ETYMOLOGY:
A British botanist, W. H. Herbert (1778–1847), who described the Rain Lily called it *pedunculata* because the long peduncle of the solitary flower is so conspicuous. The genus name honors an English botanist, Daniel Cooper (?1817–1842). Some recent workers position the species in the genus *Zephyranthes*.

Rain Lilies appear several days after a heavy rain, covering fields with their refined, white blossoms. The fragrant, night-opening flowers provide nectar for hawk moths. This species has been found to cause toxic photosensitivity in livestock. Besides that, cattle which ingest dead or dying leaves suffer a variety of symptoms including weight loss, damaged udders, and/or secondary infections.

SPECIES IN AMERICA:
About six to eight species, mostly in warm regions of U.S.A. and Mexico.

REFERENCES:

Herbert, W. H.
    1836   *Amaryllidaceae*. 179. t. 42. London: Ridgway & Sons.
Hume, H. H.
    1938   The genus *Cooperia*. Bull. Torrey Bot. Club 65:1–78.

TICKSEED

SCIENTIFIC NAME:
Coreopsis tinctoria Nuttall 1821

FAMILY:
ASTERACEAE (=COMPOSITAE)

LIFE HISTORY:
Annual herb.

ORIGIN:
Central, western United States, and Mexico.

RANGE:
West of the Mississippi River, north to Canada, west to California and south to Louisiana.

DESCRIPTION:
PLANT: Stems 1"–2' tall. Delicate leaves are divided into long, narrow segments. Upper leaves are often undivided.
FLOWER: The 8 yellow ray flowers of *Coreopsis* have 4 lobes or teeth, and those of *Thelesperma* will have 3. Flower heads are 1 to 1½" across.

BLOOM PERIOD:
May to July.

POLLINATOR(S):
Primarily larger, nectar feeding, long tongued bees, butterflies.

HABITAT REQUIREMENTS:
Moist soils of prairies and open areas. Full sun partial shade.

PROPAGATION:
Seed should be planted in the spring or fall at a recommended rate of two pounds per acre. Reseeds readily. It may also be root-divided with good results.

REMARKS & ETYMOLOGY:
The genus name combines the Greek words *kori* meaning bug (tick) and *opsis* meaning appearance, referring to the shape of the seed. *Tinctoria* means that it is used for dyeing.
   It is said that early settlers used *coreopsis* seed in their mattresses to repel ticks. This bright, easily cultivated plant is a hardy addition to the flower garden.

SPECIES IN AMERICA:
About 100 species widely distributed in warm and temperate regions.

REFERENCES:

Nuttall, T.
   1821   *J. Acad. Sci.* 2:114.
Smith, E. B.
   1976   A biosytematic survey of *Coreopsis* in eastern United States and Canada. *Sida* 6:123–215.

THORN APPLE

SCIENTIFIC NAME:
Datura wrightii Hort. ex Regel 1859

FAMILY:
SOLANACEAE

LIFE HISTORY:
Annual shrubby herb.

ORIGIN:
North America.

RANGE:
From Texas, west to California and northern Mexico.

DESCRIPTION:
PLANT: Spreading, bushy, from 2'–4' tall and 5'–8' wide.
FLOWER: Petals join to form funnel-like flower 2"–4" in diameter. Flower color white, often with pink or lavender tinge.

BLOOM PERIOD:
April to November.

POLLINATOR(S):
Hawk moth and other moths.

HABITAT REQUIREMENTS:
Found in loose sand and in moist soils of floodplains and bottomlands.

PROPAGATION:
Considered a noxious weed in most areas but the seeds are easily collected and cultivated.

REMARKS & ETYMOLOGY:
The genus name comes from the Hindu *dhatura*. All parts of this foul-smelling plant are poisonous. Dhat is the poison derived from the plant. It was described by Eduard August von Regel (1815–1892), a German botanist and director of the Botanic Garden at St. Petersburg, who named it to honor Charles Wright. In 1837 Wright went from Connecticut to survey land in central Texas for settlement, and for the next ten years he collected plants there.

Native Americans used *Datura* seeds ceremonially as intoxicants and hallucinogens. Compounds from *Datura* species have also been used pharmaceutically. The taste and smell of *Datura* is offensive to livestock. *Datura wrightii* is occasionally grown as an ornamental. The beautiful, very large trumpet-shaped corollas open only at night. An artist can trick it into "posing" for more than one day by keeping it in the refrigerator.

SPECIES IN AMERICA:
About 12 species in warm, tropical areas.

REFERENCES:

Avery, A. G., et al., eds.
1959   The Genus *Datura*. New York: The Ronald Press Co., 329.
Grant, V. & K. Grant
1983   Behavior of hawkmoths on flowers of *Datura meleloides*. *Bot. Gaz.* 144:280–84.
Regel, E. von
1856   *Gartenflora* 8:193–94; plate 260.

PURPLE CONEFLOWER

SCIENTIFIC NAME:
Echinacea purpurea Moench 1794

FAMILY:
ASTERACEAE (= COMPOSITAE)

LIFE HISTORY:
Perennial herb.

ORIGIN:
Eastern United States.

RANGE:
From northeast Texas to Oklahoma, east to Louisiana, Georgia and Missouri, and north to Ohio and Michigan.

DESCRIPTION:
PLANT: Herbaceous plant, 2'–5' tall. Coarsely-toothed leaves with rough hairs.
FLOWER: Flower heads 3"–5" diameter. Sterile ray flowers rose to deep purple. Bisexual disk flowers, often tipped with bright orange, are arranged in rounded cones.

BLOOM PERIOD:
June to October.

POLLINATOR(S):
Bees, butterflies.

HABITAT REQUIREMENTS:
Rich alkaline soils of open woods, prairies and thickets. Sun to dappled shade.

PROPAGATION:
Seed and plants are available commercially. For better germination, stratify the seed for 1–4 months before planting in the fall. Stratify by putting seeds in a moist, cool place (refrigerator). Natural stratification, alternate freezing and thawing, helps crack the seed coat. Sow seed at a rate of 12 pounds per acre. *Echinacea* can also be propagated by root divisions.

REMARKS & ETYMOLOGY:
Genus name comes from the Greek *echinos,* which means sea-urchin, referring to the prickly receptacle/basket scales. The species name, *purpurea,* describes the purple flower color. A German botanist, Conrad Moench (1744–1805), first described this plant.

Echinacea species have long been an important medicinal plant among Native Americans. Coneflowers were used to treat maladies from colds to cancer and were reported to cure venereal disease and respiratory disorders. Modern medical research suggests that E. *purpurea* helps stimulate the immune system in resisting viruses, bacteria and chemical toxins. A number of cultivars have been developed for the garden. One of these developed in England displays heads up to six or seven inches in diameter.

SPECIES IN AMERICA:
About ten in the eastern U.S.A.

REFERENCES:

Foster, S.
1985   *Echinacea* exalted: The botany, culture, history, and medical uses of the purple coneflower. Ozark Beneficial Plant Project. New Life Farm, Inc.
McGregor, R. L.
1968   The taxonomy of the genus *Echinacea* (Compositae). *Univ. Kansas Sci. Bull.* 48:113–42.
Moench, C.
1794   *Methodus plantas horti botanici et agari marburgenses* 591.

ENGELMANN'S DAISY
CUT LEAF DAISY

SCIENTIFIC NAME:
Engelmannia pinnatifida Torrey & Gray 1841

FAMILY:
ASTERACEAE (= COMPOSITAE)

LIFE HISTORY:
Perennial herb.

ORIGIN:
North America.

RANGE:
From Nebraska to Colorado, Kansas, Oklahoma, Texas, New Mexico and south to Mexico.

DESCRIPTION:
PLANT: 6″–24″ tall. Stiff hairs cover the stems and leaves. Leaves are deeply lobed.
FLOWER: Yellow flower heads, 1″–2″ diameter. Ray flowers are 3-toothed.

BLOOM PERIOD:
Late spring to summer.

POLLINATOR(S):
Solitary bees are primary; butterflies, soldier beetles.

HABITAT REQUIREMENTS:
Sandy or calcareous soils of pastures, woodlands and open coastal areas. Sun to partial sun.

PROPAGATION:
Although not always available commercially, seed can be collected in late summer. Plant in the fall.

REMARKS & ETYMOLOGY:
Two American botanists first described this prolific cut leaved daisy. Asa Gray (1810–1888) was a professor at Harvard University, while John Torrey (1796–1873) was not only a botanist, but also a chemist and physician. The generic name honors yet another American botanist, George Engelmann (1809–1884), who was of German birth. He was instrumental in establishing the scientific component of the Missouri Botanical Garden. The species name, *pinnatifida*, describes the characteristic lobed leaf.

The high protein content of Engelmann's daisy is a favored food of livestock and deer; as a result, it has been overgrazed in much of its range. This species often occurs in dense stands along roadsides. It is a long-blooming addition to your flower garden. Texas A & M University has released "El Dorado," a new Engelmann Daisy cultivar especially adapted for Texas and Oklahoma, except in the extreme eastern sections. Besides being a showy wild flower, it is a good range crop.

SPECIES IN AMERICA:
The genus contains only one species.

REFERENCES:

Torrey, J. & A. Gray
    1841   *Trans. Amer. Phil. Soc.* (n. ser.) 7:343.
Turner, B. L. & M. C. Johnston
    1956   Chromosome numbers and geographic distribution of *Lindheimera, Engelmannia,* and *Berlandiera* (Compositae, Heliantheae, Melampodinae). *Southw. Naturalist* 1:125–32.

CALIFORNIA POPPY

SCIENTIFIC NAME:
Eschscholzia californica Chamisso 1820

FAMILY:
PAPAVERACEAE

LIFE HISTORY:
Annual or perennial herb.

ORIGIN:
California.

RANGE:
Western Oregon, California and closely adjacent Mexico.

DESCRIPTION:
PLANT: Mostly 1'–2' tall; lacy leaves; stems often become prostrate with age.
FLOWER: Flowers 1"–3" in diameter, with goldish orange to yellow, cream or red petals.

BLOOM PERIOD:
February to September.

POLLINATOR(S):
Butterflies? Perhaps bees too.

HABITAT REQUIREMENTS:
Found in dry soils of grassy, open places, up to 6,500 feet. Full sun.

PROPAGATION:
Seed is widely available commercially. Plant seed from late summer to early winter. The plants reseed readily.

REMARKS & ETYMOLOGY:
The generic name honors Dr. J. F. Eschscholz (1793–1831), a Russian surgeon and naturalist with expeditions to the Pacific Coast in the early 1800s. The French-born German explorer and naturalist, Ludolf Adelbert von Chamisso (1781–1838), described the California poppy.

Spanish explorers called the golden poppy *copa de oro* or cup of gold. Native Americans of California would eat the green leaves after cooking them on hot stones. The species is highly variable, and numerous names have been proposed for this or that individual or population. Indeed, the notorious botanical "splitter," E. L. Greene (1905) recognized over 100 species for California alone. These are often referred to humorously as "chloronyms" instead of synonyms.

Eschscholzia californica is the state flower of California where showy meadows of orange poppies follow the coast.

SPECIES IN AMERICA:
About a dozen species found in western North America.

REFERENCES:

Chamisso, L. A. von
   1820   In *Horae Physicae Berolinenses*. Edited by Nees. 73. pl. 15.
Clark, C.
   1978   Systematic studies of *Eschscholzia* (Papaveraceae). I. The origin and affinities of *E. mexicana*. *Syst. Bot.* 3:374–85.
Greene, E. L.
   1905   Revision of *Eschscholtzia*. *Pittonia* 5:205–93.

PRAIRIE GENTIAN
TEXAS BLUEBELL

SCIENTIFIC NAME:
Eustoma grandiflorum (Rafinesque) 1838, Shinners, 1957

FAMILY:
GENTIANACEAE

LIFE HISTORY:
Annual, or short-lived perennial herb.

ORIGIN:
North America.

RANGE:
Found throughout most of Texas, south to Mexico and north to Oklahoma, Colorado, Kansas, and Nebraska.

DESCRIPTION:
PLANT: Several erect stems bear glaucous (with a blue-green color) foliage; 1′–2′ tall.
FLOWER: Large, showy flowers 2″–2½″ wide on pedicels up to 4″ long. Majority are blue-purple but some are white, with purple-tinged lobes, pink, and yellow.

BLOOM PERIOD:
June to September.

POLLINATOR(S):
Pollen-collecting bees, since flowers lack nectar.

HABITAT REQUIREMENTS:
Prefers moist soils of prairies, fields and drainage ditches. Full sun.

PROPAGATION:
Tiny seed is difficult to propagate, but it can be grown in a container and transplanted. Keep seeds moist until germination.

REMARKS & ETYMOLOGY:
The English botanist William J. Hooker (1785 –1865) recorded that specimens and seeds of this plant were among the last of the many novelties that were sent to the British Isles from San Felipe de Austin, Texas, in 1834 by the lamented Thomas Drummond (an early naturalist from Scotland). The wide mouth of the flower is cause for the name *Eustoma*, from the Greek meaning *eu*, good and *stoma*, mouth, given to it by Constatino Samuel Rafinesque-Schmaltz (1783–1842), from Constantinople. He was a professor of Natural History at Transylvania University in Lexington, Kentucky. Indeed, it is a *grandiflorum*, grand flower.

This large, seemingly delicate, blossom is surprisingly long-lived as a cut flower. To my surprise and relief, hard-to-find specimens used for this painting lasted up to two weeks, which recommends it to flower arrangers and florists. Japanese horticulturists have been cultivating Texas bluebell for over 70 years. The plants found in nurseries are grown in Japan. Some species of other families (e.g., *Campanula rotundifolia*) are also called blue bells, hence the name Texas Blue Bell.

SPECIES IN AMERICA:
Four or five species, mostly in Mexico.

REFERENCES:

Rafinesque, C. F.
   1838   *New Flora in North America* 4:93.
Shinners, L. H.
   1957   Synopsis of the Genus *Eustoma* (Gentianaceae). *Southw. Naturalist* 2:38–43.

INDIAN BLANKET
FIRE WHEEL
BLANKET FLOWER

SCIENTIFIC NAME:
Gaillardia pulchella Fougeroux 1786

FAMILY:
ASTERACEAE (= COMPOSITAE)

LIFE HISTORY:
Taprooted annual herb.

ORIGIN:
United States and Mexico.

RANGE:
From Nebraska, west to Colorado and south to Arizona and Mexico.

DESCRIPTION:
PLANT: Bushy, 1′–2′ tall.
FLOWER: Yellow disk flowers turn red as they open. Ray flowers (1″–2″ in diameter) are mostly red, usually tipped with yellow.

BLOOM PERIOD:
April to June.

POLLINATOR(S):
Butterflies.

HABITAT REQUIREMENTS:
Sandy or well-drained soils of prairies, fields and roadsides. Full sun.

PROPAGATION:
Indian blanket is one of the easiest wildflowers to establish. Plant seed in the fall. The recommended seeding rate is ten pounds per acre. Wear gloves while collecting seed.

REMARKS & ETYMOLOGY:
When Auguste Denis Fougeroux de Bondaroy (1732–1789) described the genus, which honors M. Gaillard de Charaentonneau, a patron of botany in France, he called the species *pulchella*, Latin for handsome.

This widespread and highly variable species was originally collected in Louisiana and sent to France about 1786 and soon after from Paris to England, where it was taken into cultivation. Forty years later, Thomas Drummond introduced various single-rayed forms of *Gaillardia pulchella* from Texas to English gardens. Originally having ray florets in a single whorl, double-whorled varieties are now available. Fields of Indian Blanket often resemble a thick, colorful carpet in late spring. An Amerindian legend associates this flower with a skillful old Indian blanket weaver who took his tapestry-making secrets to the grave. The next spring *Gaillardia* grew upon his grave, mimicking his beautiful blankets.

SPECIES IN AMERICA:
About 20 species, occurring in both North and South America.

REFERENCES:

Fougeroux, A.
    1786   *Mem. Acad. Sci. Paris* 5:1788.
Turner, B. L. & M. Whalen
    1975   Taxonomic study of *Gaillardia pulchella* (Asteraceae—Heliantheae). *Wrightia* 5:189–92.

COMMON SUNFLOWER
PRAIRIE SUNFLOWER

SCIENTIFIC NAME:
Helianthus annuus Linnaeus 1753

FAMILY:
ASTERACEAE (= COMPOSITAE)

LIFE HISTORY:
Annual herb.

ORIGIN:
Northern and central United States.

RANGE:
Widespread throughout North America.

DESCRIPTION:
PLANT: Tall plant, often reaching heights of 8'. Hairy stems are sometimes purplish.
FLOWER: Flower heads up to 5″ diameter, with sterile, yellow ray flowers surrounding brown, bisexual disk flowers.

BLOOM PERIOD:
May to October.

POLLINATOR(S):
Bees and other insects. Important source of nectar and pollen for honey bees. Butterflies not significant.

HABITAT REQUIREMENTS:
Found on dry soils of prairies, roadsides and sandy disturbed areas. Full sun.

PROPAGATION:
Seed is commonly available. Many hybrids are on the market as well. Sow seed in fall or spring.

REMARKS & ETYMOLOGY:
The genus name comes from the Greek words *helios* (sun) and *anthos* (flower), while the species name indicates that it is an annual. The species was first described by Linnaeus.

The sunflower has long been part of mythologies and rituals. The Incas of Peru worshipped sunflowers as symbols of the sun.

All parts of the sunflower have practical uses: the seeds provide food for humans and wildlife, the flowers can be used in dyes, the stalks are a source of fiber and paper pulp, and the oil is highly prized economically. The huge sunflower cultivated commercially is the result of hundreds of years of cultivation by the Native Americans, but was perfected in Europe and Russia. Today, there are numerous cultivars grown for seed, fodder, and ornamentals. All sunflowers are native to America and the common sunflower is believed to have originated in midwestern North America. Sunflowers are among the first plants to grow in abandoned fields but their stay is brief because the toxin they release into the soil inhibits the growth of neighboring plants as well as that of its own seedlings. The annual habit is unusual among sunflowers. The sunflower's tolerance to smoke probably accounts for its success in industrial areas.

SPECIES IN AMERICA:
About 70 species in North America

REFERENCES:

Heiser, C. B.
    1976   *The Sunflower*. Norman: University of Oklahoma Press.
Linnaeus, C.
    1753   *Species Plantarum* 906.
Rogers, C. E., T. E. Thompson, & G. J. Seiler
    1982   *Sunflower species of the United States*. Bismarck, ND: National Sunflower Assoc.

MAXIMILIAN SUNFLOWER

SCIENTIFIC NAME:
Helianthus maximiliani Schrader 1835

FAMILY:
ASTERACEAE (= COMPOSITAE)

LIFE HISTORY:
Perennial herb.

ORIGIN:
North America.

RANGE:
Southern Canada, south to Texas and east to North Carolina.

DESCRIPTION:
PLANT: Erect with several unbranched stems 1'–8' tall. Short, rough hairs cover the stems and leaves, which make them sticky to the touch.
FLOWER: Yellow ray flowers are sterile; reddish brown or purple disk flowers. Flower heads up to 4" across. Rays always cupped; no other sunflower has this characteristic.

BLOOM PERIOD:
Late summer to fall.

POLLINATOR(S):
Butterflies, bees.

HABITAT REQUIREMENTS:
Prefers moist clay soils of prairies, depressions and drainage ditches. Full sun.

PROPAGATION:
By division or seeding. Divide the rootstock in early spring, and replant immediately. Seed in early winter. Rake seed into loose topsoil or cover lightly with soil or mulch. Seed is available commercially.

REMARKS & ETYMOLOGY:
The generic name is from the Greek words *helios* (sun) and *anthos* (flower). The specific name honors the German prince Maximilian Philip, who participated in scientific expeditions to North America in the 1830s. The American plant was first described by German botanist Heinrich Adolph Schrader (1767–1836).

Sunflowers are palatable to livestock and wildlife. Maximilian's sunflower is closely related to *H. tuberosus* (Jerusalem artichoke), which produces edible tubers that were an important component in the diets of native Americans in North America. It blooms later than *H. annuus*, and its glowing yellow clusters have landscape potential as a fall perennial.

SPECIES IN AMERICA:
About 70 species, all native to North America.

REFERENCES:

Heiser, C. B., Jr.
    1976   *The Sunflower.* Norman: University of Oklahoma Press.
Rogers, C. E., T. E. Thompson & G. J. Seiler
    1982   *Sunflower species of the United States.* Bismark, ND: National Sunflower Assoc.
Schrader, H. A.
    1835   *Ind. Sem. Hort. Gotting. Ex. Ann. Sci. Nat.* Ser. 2. 6:101.

SPIDERLILY

SCIENTIFIC NAME:
Hymenocallis liriosme (Rafinesque) 1838, Shinners 1951

FAMILY:
AMARYLLIDACEAE

LIFE HISTORY:
Perennial bulbous herb.

ORIGIN:
North America.

RANGE:
From Louisiana to Texas, and north to Arkansas and Missouri.

DESCRIPTION:
PLANT: Upright fleshy or succulent, to 3' tall. Thick, spongy stems are sharply two-edged. Wide, glossy leaves are 6"–30" long.
FLOWER: Flowers 7" diameter, white, tinged with yellow, 4 to 6 in a cluster. Stamens are joined by a thin membrane. Sepals and petals are identical and are collectively referred to as tepals.

BLOOM PERIOD:
March to May.

POLLINATOR(S):
Probably hawk moths.

HABITAT REQUIREMENTS:
Moist soils of stream banks, ditches, and wet areas. Shade to part sun.

PROPAGATION:
Divide small bulbs from the base of larger (4"–5" diameter) bulbs.

REMARKS & ETYMOLOGY:
Spiderlily stamens are united by a delicate membrane, hence the generic name, *Hymenocallis*, from the Greek *hymen* (membrane) and *kallos* (beauty). Constantin Samuel Rafinesque-Schmaltz (1783–1840), who was born in Constantinople but became a professor in America, first described the Spiderlily. It was transferred to the genus *Hymenocallis* by Lloyd Herbert Shinners (1918–1971), a Canadian-born botanist and professor at Southern Methodist University, Dallas.

The big, white flowers are very, very fragrant, which suggests a night visiting pollinator to this hardy plant, which readily adapts to gardens.

SPECIES IN AMERICA:
Over 40 species in warm areas of the Western Hemisphere.

REFERENCES:

Rafinesque, C. S.
    1838   *Flora ludoviciana* 19.
Shinners, L. H.
    1951   The North Texas Species of *Hymenocallis* (Amaryllidaceae). *Field & Lab.* 19:102–04.

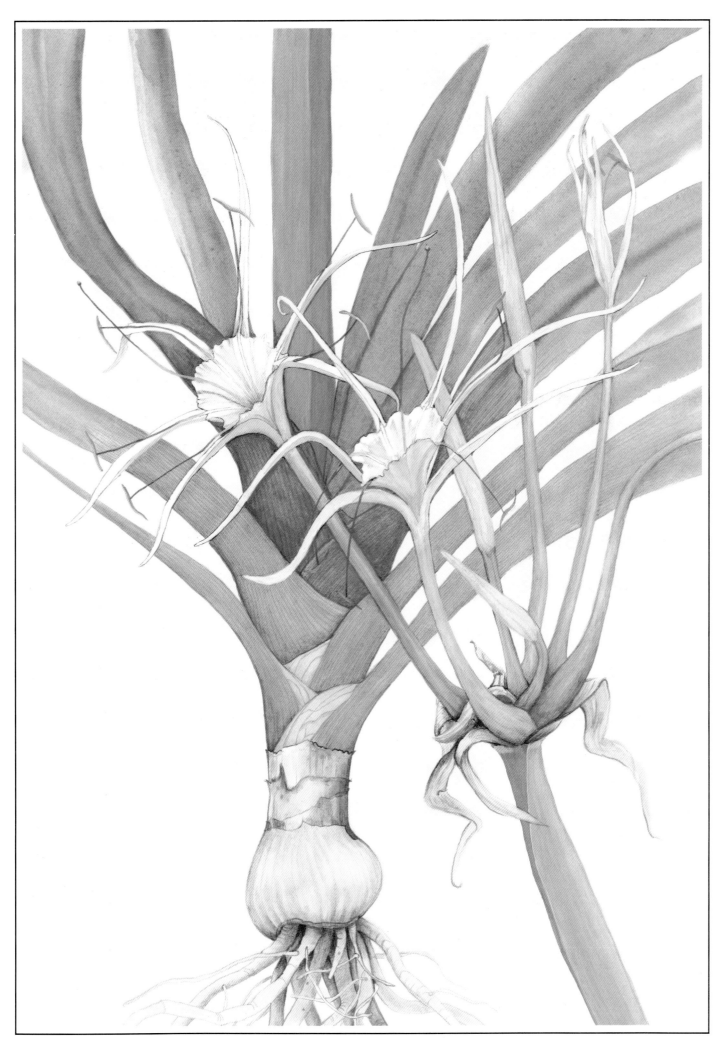

PURPLE BIND WEED
WILD MORNING GLORY

SCIENTIFIC NAME:
Ipomoea cordatotriloba Dennstedt 1810

FAMILY:
CONVOLVULACEAE

LIFE HISTORY:
Perennial twining herb.

ORIGIN:
Southeastern United States.

RANGE:
Southeastern states, Kansas, Texas, and Mexico.

DESCRIPTION:
PLANT: Low-climbing, twining vine. Leaves variable, unlobed or 3-lobed; 1″–1½″ long.
FLOWER: Pink or purple funnel-shaped corollas with a deep purple-red throat, 1″–1½″ long x 2″ wide.

BLOOM PERIOD:
April to October.

POLLINATOR(S):
Hummingbirds, probably.

HABITAT REQUIREMENTS:
Sandy coastal plain; a weed in cultivated ground or waste places.

PROPAGATION:
Seed or by root division. Can become obnoxious in a garden.

REMARKS:
This tenacious invader was long known as *I. trichocarpa*, so-named by the South Carolinian Stephen Elliot (1771–1830) in 1817. However, recent workers have shown that it had received an earlier name, *I. cordatotrilobata*. *Ipomoea*, from the Greek *ips*, a worm that eats vines, in reference to the worm-like climbing stems. *Cordato* refers to the heart shape of the 3-lobed leaves, *triloba* named by August Wilhelm Dennstedt (1776–1826), a German physican and botanist who was director of the Belvedere garden near Weimar, Germany.

Although the flower is quite pretty, the vine can quickly overrun a flower bed.

SPECIES IN AMERICA:
About 40; over 600 in warm-temperate and tropical regions of both hemispheres.

REFERENCES:

Austin, D. F.
1976   Nomenclatural changes in *Ipomoea batatas. Taxon* 37:184–85.
1988   Varieties of *Ipomoea trichocarpa* (Convolulaceae). *Sida* 6:216–20.
Dennstedt, A. W.
1810   *Nomencl. Bat.* 1: 246.
Elliot, S.
1817   *A sketch of the botany of South Carolina and Georgia.*

STANDING CYPRESS
TEXAS PLUME

SCIENTIFIC NAME:
Ipomopsis rubra (Nuttall) 1818, Wherry 1936

FAMILY:
POLEMONIACEAE

LIFE HISTORY:
Biennial herb.

ORIGIN:
Southern United States.

RANGE:
From Texas, east to Florida and north to North Carolina.

DESCRIPTION:
PLANT: Single, unbranched stem, 1′–4′ tall. Leaves, ½″ long and divided into numerous thread-like segments.
FLOWER: Flowers, orange-red in color, are in clusters at the top of the stem. Five petals join to form a tube.

BLOOM PERIOD:
Summer to fall.

POLLINATOR(S):
Hummingbirds.

HABITAT REQUIREMENTS:
Prefers dry, sandy or rocky soils of fields, roadsides and woodland edges. Sun to partial shade.

PROPAGATION:
Seeds germinate readily. Plant seeds in the fall. Recommended seeding rate for large scale planting is six pounds per acre. The plants will form a leafy rosette the first season, then bolt and flower the second year.

REMARKS & ETYMOLOGY:
Edgar Theodore Wherry (1885–1982), who transferred Standing Cypress into the genus *Ipomopsis* (it was originally placed by Nuttall in the genus *Gilia*), was an American botanist, mineralogist and chemist. The genus name, *Ipomopsis* means "looks like a worm," referring to the plant's narrow, sometimes twisting form. The species name, *rubra,* refers to the flowers' red color.

The blossoms last well as cut flowers. It is often cultivated, and grouped plantings are spectacular.

SPECIES IN AMERICA:
About 25 species, mostly in the southwestern United States.

REFERENCES:

Grant, V.
    1956   A synopsis of *Ipomopsis. El Aliso* 3:351–62.
Nuttall, T.
    1818   *Gen. N. Amer. Pl.* 1:124–25.
Wherry, E. T.
    1936   Miscellaneous eastern *Polemoniaceae. Bartonia* 18:52–59.

69

LOUISIANA IRIS
RED FLAG
RED IRIS

SCIENTIFIC NAME:
Iris fulva Ker-Gawler 1812

FAMILY:
IRIDACEAE

LIFE HISTORY:
Rhizomatous perennial.

ORIGIN:
Eastern and northern United States.

RANGE:
From Georgia, east to Louisiana and into Texas, north to Arkansas, Missouri, Kentucky and Ohio.

DESCRIPTION:
PLANT: Thick rhizomes (underground stems). Basal, linear leaves are about 3′ long.
FLOWER: Flower stalk up to 5′ tall. Flowers copper to reddish orange, 1″–3″ long. Sepals are longer than petals.

BLOOM PERIOD:
March to May.

POLLINATOR(S):
Bees.

HABITAT REQUIREMENTS:
Prefers acidic, alluvial soils, rich in organic matter. Grows in open areas of cypress and hardwood swamps, along stream banks, roadside ditches and seepage areas. Needs full sun to part shade. Cannot tolerate brackish water.

PROPAGATION:
Louisiana iris can readily be propagated asexually from the rhizomes. Divide the parent plant in late summer or early fall. Transplant the divisions immediately and water thoroughly. Old rhizomes can be cut and placed in flats to initiate additional plants. New shoots will sprout along the length of the rhizome. Irises can also be propagated from seed.

REMARKS & ETYMOLOGY:
The genus name associates the multicolored hues of the flowers with Iris, the Greek goddess of the rainbow. The species name, *fulva*, describes the tawny, copper color of this particular one. The author of this species, John Bellenden Ker, 1765?–1842, (first known as John Gawler) was an enigmatic British botanist, wit, and man of fashion, who edited *Edward's Botanical Register* before he came to America.

The iris has long been a symbol of royalty and heraldry, as seen in the *fleur-de-lis*. The roots, used medicinally by Native Americans, easily adapt to cultivation.

SPECIES IN AMERICA:
Over 200 species in North America.

REFERENCES:

Caillet, M. & J. K. Mertzweiller
   1988   *The Louisiana Iris: the history and culture of five native American species and their hybrids.* Waco, TX: Texas Gardener Press.
Ker, J. B.
   1812   *Bot. Mag.* t. 1496.

TEXAS LANTANA
HIERBA DE CRISTO

SCIENTIFIC NAME:
Lantana horrida von Humboldt [Bonpland & Kunth]
1815

FAMILY:
VERBENACEAE

LIFE HISTORY:
Perennial shrub.

ORIGIN:
Tropical and Subtropical America.

RANGE:
Thoughout most of Texas to California, northern
Mexico, introduced and established in southeastern
states. Louisiana, Mississippi and Mexico; widely cultivated elsewhere and frequently escaping.

DESCRIPTION:
PLANT: Shrubs 3′–6′ tall. Erect, spreading branches
with rough, dark green leaves.
FLOWER: Many-flowered heads, 1″–3″ in diameter.
Flower colors orange, yellow and red mixed.

BLOOM PERIOD:
Spring to fall.

POLLINATOR(S):
Butterflies, bees.

HABITAT REQUIREMENTS:
Fields, thickets, hillsides, swamps and roadsides. Full
to part sun.

PROPAGATION:
Seed can be collected after fruit has filled out and
turned dark, usually late summer or early fall. Dry
seeds before storing. Plant in spring or fall. Lantana can also be propagated from softwood or semi-
hardwood cuttings. Take cuttings in summer. Root
cuttings can be taken in late winter. *Lantana horrida* and
yet other species have been cultivated, and are available
in commercial nurseries.

REMARKS & ETYMOLOGY:
The generic name *lantana* is derived from the Latin
meaning *viburnum*, which its flowering branches
superficially resemble. Fredrick Wilhelm Heinrich
Alexander von Humboldt (1769–1859), a famous German geographer and traveler throughout tropical
America, described this plant, along with Bonpland
and Kunth, from a Mexican specimen. The species received the name, *horrida*, presumably because of the
harsh, unpleasant to the touch, foliage or perhaps because of the pungent, unpleasant odor emitted when
its leaves are crushed.

Extremely drought-tolerant, species of *Lantana*
make an excellent choice for dry landscapes. Many
cultivars, including trailing and dwarf types, have been
selected. With a little water, lantanas will bloom for
most of the year. Use caution when planting them because the berries are highly toxic. Plant them out of
the reach of small children, for deaths have been reported when the mature succulent fruits are consumed
in large numbers. The leaves contain the alkaloid lan-
tanine, which can be used to reduce fevers. Livestock
avoid the plant. Lantana was introduced to Australia
where it has literally "taken over" and become a pest.
It has also escaped to roadsides in Thailand and Indonesia, where it was introduced to gardens and to attract butterflies at a butterfly "farm." Since its sixteenth-century introduction, the trailing lantana bush
now reaches twenty or thirty feet tall in many of In-
dia's "jungles." Many birds such as Tickell's Flower-
pecker have become dependent on their berries, and
thus they have been spread throughout the sub-
continent.

SPECIES IN AMERICA:
About 160 species, mostly in tropical and subtropical
America.

REFERENCES:

Correll, D. S. and M. C. Johnston
    1970   *Lantana,* in *Manual of Vascular Plants of Texas.* Texas Research Foundation, Renner, Texas.
Humboldt, F. A. von
    1815   *Nova genera et species plantarum* 261.

GAYFEATHER
BLAZING STAR

SCIENTIFIC NAME:
Liatris punctata Hooker 1834

FAMILY:
ASTERACEAE (=COMPOSITAE)

LIFE HISTORY:
Perennnial herb.

ORIGIN:
Southern and eastern United States.

RANGE:
Probably the widest range of any species of the genus, extending from about the 53rd parallel in western Canada, south to northern Mexico, though not east of the Mississippi.

DESCRIPTION:
PLANT: 1'–3' tall, stems single or in clusters from corm-like rootstocks.
FLOWER: Plume-like with flowers arranged in cylindrical groups at tops of branches, pink to purple in color. Florets ⅜″–½″ long.

BLOOM PERIOD:
July to October.

POLLINATOR(S):
Butterflies, bees.

HABITAT REQUIREMENTS:
Prefers well-drained calcareous soils of prairies and fields. Full sun.

PROPAGATION:
Divide corms in late fall or early spring. Separate corms with a sharp knife and replant. *Liatris* can also be grown from seed. Sow in the fall to allow for stratification period.

REMARKS & ETYMOLOGY:
In the early days of "botanizing" in the United States, William Jackson Hooker (1785–1865), as the director of the Royal Botanic Gardens at Kew, England, received many American plants which he had the honor to name and describe. The derivation of *Liatris* is unknown, but *punctata* refers to the minute pits or dots on vegetative parts.

Gayfeather makes an excellent cut flower, and also dries well. It is cultivated and widely used by commercial florists. The edible, corm-like roots were a staple in the diet of many Native Americans. Because of its deep corm-like roots, gayfeather can withstand extreme droughts and often grows in impossible looking, rocky situations.

SPECIES IN AMERICA:
About 40 species in America

REFERENCES:

Gaiser, L. O.
1946   The genus *Liatris. Rhodora* 48:165–83; 216–412.
Hooker, W. J.
1834   *Flora Boreali-Americana.* 1:306. t. 105. London: Treuttel & Wurtz.

BLUE FLAX
PRAIRIE FLAX

SCIENTIFIC NAME:
Linum lewisii Pursh 1814

FAMILY:
LINACEAE

LIFE HISTORY:
Perennial herb.

ORIGIN:
North America.

RANGE:
From Alaska, south to California, Texas and northern Mexico.

DESCRIPTION:
PLANT: Sprawling, 18″–20″ tall, with narrow leaves.
FLOWER: Pale blue flowers, 1″–2″ diameter, with darker blue veins. Several flowers per stem.

BLOOM PERIOD:
April to September.

POLLINATOR(S):
Bees.

HABITAT REQUIREMENTS:
Found on sandy or rocky slopes. Part shade to full sun.

PROPAGATION:
Seed is widely available commercially. Grows on a variety of well-drained soils.

REMARKS & ETYMOLOGY:
The genus name, *Linum*, is Latin for flax. Frederick T. Pursh (1774–1820), a German botanist who lived in the United States for twelve years, named the species to honor Captain Meriwether Lewis (1774–1809), a nineteenth-century American explorer of the Lewis and Clark expedition across the Rocky Mountains.

The tough, fibrous, stems of this delicate-looking flower were used in making rope and fishing lines. The seeds contain linseed oil, a component of paints and varnishes. Medicinally, flax serves as a laxative or can be used to treat burns.

SPECIES IN AMERICA:
About 150 species in tropical and temperate regions.

REFERENCES:

Mosquin, T.
  1971   Biosytematic studies in the North American species of *Linum*, section *Adenolinum* (Linaceae). *Canad. J. Bot.* 49:1379–88.
Pursh, F. T.
  1814   *Flora Americae Septentrionalis* 1:210.
Rogers, C. M.
  1969   Relationships of the North American species of *Linum*. *Bull. Torrey Bot. Club* 96:176–90.

TRUMPET HONEYSUCKLE

SCIENTIFIC NAME:
Lonicera sempervirens Linnaeus 1753

FAMILY:
CAPRIFOLIACEAE

LIFE HISTORY:
Perennial woody vine.

ORIGIN:
North America.

RANGE:
Throughout much of eastern United States.

DESCRIPTION:
PLANT: Twining shrub with smooth shiny leaves and branches.
FLOWER: Bright red trumpet-like flowers in whorls of 4 to 6. Showy red fruit follows.

BLOOM PERIOD:
Spring to summer.

POLLINATOR(S):
Hummingbirds, butterflies.

HABITAT REQUIREMENTS:
Grows in woods and thickets, near ponds or in moist areas.

PROPAGATION:
Seeds need to be stratified in order to germinate. Sow in the fall. Softwood or semi-hardwood cuttings can be taken from summer to fall.

REMARKS & ETYMOLOGY:
The genus name honors Adam Lonitzer (1528–1586), a German physician and naturalist. The species name, *sempervirens*, means evergreen.

Not overly aggressive as is its cousin *L. albiflora*, the colorful trumpet honeysuckle grows well on fences or trellises. The scarlet flowers are showy and long-lasting, attracting birds and other wildlife which eat the fruit, thereby assuring seed dispersal. Native Americans as well as hunters and miners also used the fruit as food.

SPECIES IN AMERICA:
About 40 species in temperate and sub-tropical regions.

REFERENCES:

Linnaeus, C.
　1753　　　　*Species Plantarum* 173.
Rehder, A.
　1903　　　　Synopsis of the genus *Lonicera. Annual Rep. Missouri Bot. Gard.* 14:27–232.

TEXAS BLUEBONNET

SCIENTIFIC NAME:
Lupinus texensis Hooker 1836

FAMILY:
FABACEAE (= LEGUMINOSAE)

LIFE HISTORY:
Annual herb.

ORIGIN:
Texas.

RANGE:
Throughout most of Texas; widely planted along roadsides by the Texas Department of Transportation.

DESCRIPTION:
PLANT: Erect or sprawling, 6″–16″ tall. Stems branch from base. Leaves alternate, blades divided into 5 leaflets.
FLOWER: Many irregular flowers in a dense terminal raceme. Flowers blue with a white spot on upper petal that turns magenta with age.

BLOOM PERIOD:
March to May.

POLLINATOR(S):
Pollen-collecting bees, since flowers lack nectar.

HABITAT REQUIREMENTS:
Sandy or calcareous soils in prairies, pastures and hill-sides. Full sun.

PROPAGATION:
Plant seed in well-drained soil in the fall. Because of the hard seed coat, the seed may not germinate the first year or more. Recommended seeding rate about 30 pounds per acre. Although most soils contain *Rhizobium* bacteria, dusting the seed with an innoculant (powder containing *Rhizobium)* before planting insures the presence of that nitrogen-producing symbiotic bacterium, essential for the formation of root nodules and the consequent plant growth and bloom. Do not fertilize. Added fertilizer affects the bacterial development of nodules thereby reducing the number of blooms per plant.

REMARKS & ETYMOLOGY:
The genus name, *Lupinus*, is Latin for wolf. Early botanists, seeing lush lupines growing in poor soil deduced that the plants devoured soil nutrients as the wolf devours its prey. To the contrary, lupines have the ability to produce nitrogen which enhances the soil.

Although 200 species of lupines may be found throughout the world, nowhere are they so loved as in Texas. The Texan takes his/her state flower seriously. The blue flower blankets the roadsides and fields of Texas in the spring, making a pilgrimage to that state in late March or early April worthwhile.

SPECIES IN AMERICA:
About 200 species worldwide in temperate regions.

REFERENCES:

Andrews, J.
   1987   *The Texas Bluebonnet.* Austin: Univ. Texas Press.
Crank, E.
   1988   Effects of fertilizer on *Rhizobium* nodulation in *Lupinus texensis. Wildflower: J. National Wildflower Research Center* 1:27–31.
Hooker, W. J.
   1836   *Bot. Mag.* 63: t. 3492.
Schaal, B. A.
   1980   Pollination and banner markings in *Lupinus texensis* (Leguminosae). *Southw. Naturalist,* 25:280–81.
Shinners, L. H.
   1953   The bluebonnets (*Lupinus*) of Texas. *Field & Lab.* 21:49–153.

TURK'S CAP
TEXAS WAX MALLOW

SCIENTIFIC NAME:
Malvaviscus arboreus Cavanilles 1793

FAMILY:
MALVACEAE

LIFE HISTORY:
Perennial shrub or small tree.

ORIGIN:
Caribbean Islands.

RANGE:
Florida to Texas, Caribbean Islands, Mexico south to Venezuela, widely introduced elsewhere in gardens.

DESCRIPTION:
PLANT: Medium to large shrub, 2'–4' high, with many-branched, woody stems; can form dense colonies along stream banks.
FLOWER: Red petals (1"–2" long) curl and overlap so as to form a turban-like corolla. Red berry-like fruit is produced in the fall.

BLOOM PERIOD:
May to frost.

POLLINATOR(S):
Hummingbirds pollinate; butterflies and bees rob nectar.

HABITAT REQUIREMENTS:
Prefers moist soils of woods, stream and river banks. Also found on limestone slopes and ledges. Partial shade.

PROPAGATION:
Seed can be collected as soon as the fruit is ripe. Dry fruit until pulp begins to shrivel. Plant seed after danger of frost has passed. Stem cuttings can be taken from summer soft wood, or rootstock may be divided.

REMARKS & ETYMOLOGY:
The genus name combines the Latin name for the mallow with *viscus* (glue), which refers to the pulp around the seeds. *Arboreus* refers to its often tree-like character, especially in tropical regions. The author, Antonio Jose Cavanilles (1745–1804), was a Spanish botanist.

The round, red Turk's cap fruit is edible, raw or cooked. Turk's cap is a good choice for shady areas in warmer climes, but it can become aggressive. I have seen it as an escapee from introduced cultivation in Australia, Thailand, and throughout Indonesia. Native suffruticose populations in the southeastern United States have been designated as var. *drummondii*; in more tropical areas the species becomes a shrub or small tree.

SPECIES IN AMERICA:
About 5 species.

Cavanilles, A. J.
    1787   *Tert. Diss. Bot.* 3, t. 48.
Schery, R. W.
    1942   Monograph of *Malvaviscus. Ann. Missouri Bot. Gard.* 29:183–244.
Turner, B. L. & M. G. Mendenhall
    1992   A revision of *Malvaviscus* (Malavaceae). *Ann. Missouri Bot. Gard.* (in press).

LEMON MINT
HORSEMINT
BEEBALM

SCIENTIFIC NAME:
Monarda citriodora Cervantes 1816

FAMILY:
LAMIACEAE (= LABIATAE)

LIFE HISTORY:
Annual or biennial herb.

ORIGIN:
Southern United States and Mexico.

RANGE:
Missouri and Kansas, south to Texas and northeastern Mexico.

DESCRIPTION:
PLANT: 1'–3' tall; several stems arise from base; can form large colonies over several acres. Stems are square.
FLOWER: Two-lipped, about ¾" long, usually lavender, pink, or white.

BLOOM PERIOD:
April to October.

POLLINATOR:
Nectar-collecting bees, bumble bees, and wasps; hummingbirds and butterflies visit but are not major pollinators.

HABITAT REQUIREMENTS:
Found in sandy loam or rocky soils on slopes and hills or prairies and meadows. Full sun to partial shade.

PROPAGATION:
Easily grown by seed. Spread the seed evenly and rake into loose topsoil. Recommended seeding rate is 3 pounds per acre. Allow seeds to mature fully (will turn brown and dry) before mowing or collecting. Reseeds readily.

REMARKS & ETYMOLOGY:
The genus honors Nicolas Monardes (1493–1588), a late sixteenth-century Spanish herbalist who specialized in New World plants. A Mexican botanist, Vincente de Cervantes (1759?–1829), authored the species.

When "horse" is used in plant names it often refers to coarseness. Since Lemon Mint has a distinct citrus fragrance when crushed, the species name derives from the Latin *citrus* (lemon tree) and *odoro* (having a fragrant smell).

The leaves make a delicate tea. This herb was eaten with meat by the Hopi Indians of Arizona. Lemon mint contains an aromatic compound, citronellol, which is extracted to use as an insect repellent. This genus has many showy domesticated cultivars. The fragrance and hummingbird-attracting qualities, along with its striking blossom, recommend this hardy plant to the gardener.

SPECIES IN AMERICA:
About 20 species. Several are in cultivation and others are worthy of it.

REFERENCES:

Lagasca y Segura, M.
    1816   *Genera et species plantarum novarum 2.*
McClintock, E. & C. Epling
    1942   A review of the genus *Monarda* (Labiatae). *Univ. Calif. Publ. Bot.* 20:147–94.

FRAGRANT WATER LILY
ALLIGATOR BONNET

SCIENTIFIC NAME:
Nymphaea odorata Solander 1786

FAMILY:
NYMPHAEACEAE

LIFE HISTORY:
Perennial aquatic herb.

ORIGIN:
Eastern United States.

RANGE:
From Florida to Texas, and north to Canada, as far west as Manitoba.

DESCRIPTION:
PLANT: Large (to 10″ diameter), round, bright green leaves, red or purplish underneath, float on top of the water.
FLOWER: The flowers, usually one per stem, have four petal-like sepals and many rows of white petals (sometimes over 25). Numerous yellow stamens. Very fragrant.

BLOOM PERIOD:
March to October.

POLLINATOR(S):
Bees, butterflies.

HABITAT REQUIREMENTS:
Still waters of ponds, lakes, slow streams and ditches.

PROPAGATION:
Divide rhizomes in early fall, and replant divisions. Prefers deep, rich mud in slow-moving water. Do not expose roots to drying.

REMARKS & ETYMOLOGY:
Called *Nympheaea* after one of the water nymphs of Greek mythology, water lilies are further described as being scented because the flowers are not only very handsome but extremely fragrant. Daniel Solander (1733–1782) described this species in a journal edited by William Aiton at Kew, England. Solander was an adventurous Swedish botanist who accompanied Joseph Banks on the voyage of Capt. Cook's *Endeavor* (1768–1771).

Water lilies are considered by many botanists to be one of the most primitive of living plants. The flower opens and closes for several days until pollinated. The fleshy young leaves and flower buds can be boiled and eaten as vegetables. In the past some people used various parts of the plants medicinally to treat such ailments as skin blemishes and baldness, while others thought they could counteract witchcraft.

SPECIES IN AMERICA:
N. mexicana, N. elegans, N. tuberosa

REFERENCES:

St. John, H.
1942   The water lily, *Nymphaea odorata. Leafl. W. Bot.* 3:142–44.
Solander, D.
1789   In Aiton's *Hortus Kewensis.* ed. I, 2:227.

MISSOURI EVENING PRIMROSE FLUTTERMILL

SCIENTIFIC NAME:
Oenothera missouriensis Sims 1813

FAMILY:
ONAGRACEAE

LIFE HISTORY:
Biennial or short-lived (up to 3 years) perennial herb.

ORIGIN:
Central United States.

RANGE:
From Texas to Oklahoma, Arkansas, Missouri, Kansas and Nebraska.

DESCRIPTION:
PLANT: Usually several stems arise from the base. Reaches heights of 4″–18″. Long, narrow leaves.
FLOWER: Large, yellow flowers up to 4″ diameter. Large seed capsules have four broad wings.

BLOOM PERIOD:
May to August.

POLLINATOR(S):
Hawk moths; small bees and beetles scavenge pollen.

HABITAT REQUIREMENTS:
Found in dry, rocky, limestone soils of prairies, cliffs and hillsides. Full sun.

PROPAGATION:
Seed can be collected from pods and sown in the fall. Missouri primrose grows well in rock gardens, where its trailing stems can droop gracefully.

REMARKS & ETYMOLOGY:
Oenothera from *oinothera*, the Greek name for a kind of plant with roots that smell like wine. The species honors the state where it was first found. It was described by John Sims (1749–1831), a British physician and botanist.

Like other members of the evening primrose family, Missouri primrose opens at dusk and closes in the morning. This habit is hard on the artist wishing to paint the open flower. The pale flowers with a sweet scent attract night pollinators. It was introduced long ago to English and European gardens, where it is a popular cultivated flower. The dried, winged capsules or fruits make engaging additions to dried flower arrangements.

SPECIES IN AMERICA:
About 80 species in temperate zones of the Americas.

REFERENCES:

Munz, P. A.
1930   Studies in Onagraceae V. The North American species of the subgenera *Lavauxia* and *Megapterium* of the genus *Oenothera*. *Amer. J. Bot.* 17:358–70.
Raven, P. H.
1962   The systematics of *Oenothera* subgenus *Chylismia*. *Univ. Calif. Publ. Bot.* 34:1–122.
Sims, J.
1813   *Bot. Mag.*, t. 1592.
Wagner, W. L.
1983   New species and combination in the genus *Oenothera* (Onagraceae). *Ann. Missouri Bot. Gard.* 70:194–96.

89

PINK EVENING PRIMROSE
SHOWY PINK PRIMROSE

SCIENTIFIC NAME:
Oenothera speciosa Nuttall 1821

FAMILY:
ONAGRACEAE

LIFE HISTORY:
Perennial herb.

ORIGIN:
South-central United States.

RANGE:
Missouri to Kansas and south to Texas and Mexico.

DESCRIPTION:
PLANT: Upright or sprawling herbaceous plant, to 2′ tall. Plants spread by underground running rootstock.
FLOWER: Pink to white in color, 2″–3″ in diameter.

BLOOM PERIOD:
April to July.

POLLINATOR(S):
Most members of this family open at night and are pollinated by moths and night insects; also by bees and hummingbirds.

HABITAT REQUIREMENTS:
Various soils of prairies and open woodlands. Full sun.

PROPAGATION:
Although field seedings have had mixed success, this species germinates readily indoors. Seed is available in limited quantities. Suggested seeding rate is one half pound per acre. Once established, it will take over the place if not controlled.

REMARKS & ETYMOLOGY:
The generic name *Oenothera* derives from *oinothera*, the Greek name for a kind of plant with roots that smell like wine; the specific name is derived from Latin *speciosa* meaning beautiful or showy. The author of this species, Thomas Nuttall (1786–1859), was a British naturalist and early botanical explorer of the United States.

Unlike many evening primroses which open at night, pink evening primrose blooms during the day in its southern range. It is not related to the true primrose (*Primula*). The clear pink wildflower occurs in vast, showy masses which make it desirable in field plantings, especially along highways. Because of this, the Pink Evening Primrose has been adopted as the symbol of the National Wildflower Research Center, which is housed in Austin, Texas.

SPECIES IN AMERICA:
About 80 species in North and South America.

REFERENCES:

Munz, P. A.
1932   Studies in Onagraceae VII. The North American species of the subgenera *Hartmannia* and *Gauropsis* of the genus *Oenothera*. The genus *Gayophytumn*. *Amer. J. Bot.* 19:764–65.
Nuttall, T.
1821   *J. Phil. Acad. Sci.* 2:119.
Raven, P. H. & D .R. Parnell
1970   Two new species and nomenclatural changes in *Oenothera* subgenus *Hartmannia* (*Onagraceae*). *Madroño* 20:246–49.

CORN POPPY
FIELD POPPY
FLANDERS POPPY

SCIENTIFIC NAME:
Papaver rhoeas Linnaeus 1753

FAMILY:
PAPAVERACEAE

LIFE HISTORY:
Annual herb.

ORIGIN:
Eastern regions about the Mediterranean Sea.

RANGE:
Naturalized from Europe and widely introduced elsewhere.

DESCRIPTION:
PLANT: Erect, branched; 2′–4′ tall.
FLOWER: Flowers orange-red, purple, scarlet, or occasionally white. Flower 2″ diameter.

BLOOM PERIOD:
Spring to summer.

POLLINATOR(S):
Pollen-collecting bees

HABITAT REQUIREMENTS:
Found in various soils of fields, roadsides and open areas. Full sun to partial shade.

PROPAGATION:
Seeds are often part of commercial wildflower mixes. Sow seed in spring or fall.

REMARKS & ETYMOLOGY:
An Old World plant that was described by the "Father of Botany" Carolus Linnaeus. *Rhoeas* is an old Greek name of obscure derivation, but *Papaver* is Latin for poppy.

The common field poppy of Europe is often called Flanders poppy, alluding to a World War I poem by John McCrae that mentions poppies in Flanders Fields. In that spirit it is also called the Veteran's Poppy and is worn on World War I Armistice Day. The flowers have some medicinal properties, while the pigments are used to color medicines and wine. Early European colonists introduced the plant to America, where it naturalized readily.

SPECIES IN AMERICA:
About 100 species in the North Temperate Zones of Eurasia and North America.

REFERENCES:

Kadereit, J. W.
    1990   Some suggestions on the geographical origin of the central, west, and north European synathropic species of *Papaver* L. *Bot. J. Linn. Soc.* 103:221–31.
Linnaeus, C.
    1753   *Species Plantarum* 507.

JEAN ANDREWS

PASSION FLOWER
MAY POP

SCIENTIFIC NAME:
Passiflora incarnata Linnaeus 1753

FAMILY:
PASSIFLORACEAE

LIFE HISTORY:
Tender perennial climber.

ORIGIN:
Southern United States.

RANGE:
From Virginia to Missouri south to Florida and Texas.

DESCRIPTION:
PLANT: Herbaceous vine, erect, trailing or climbing, to 25′ long. Alternate leaves deeply lobed, 3″–5″ long, with two nectar glands at the base of each blade.
FLOWER: Lavender or purple petals and sepals, beneath a fringe of white or purple filaments. Flowers 2″–3″ diameter.

BLOOM PERIOD:
April to August.

POLLINATOR(S):
Butterflies, bees, and other insects.

HABITAT REQUIREMENTS:
Rich, heavy soils of old fields, roadsides, stream banks and open woods. Full sun.

PROPAGATION:
Collect the yellow fruits to obtain seed. Seeds should be firm and brown. Seed often has low viability, and germination can take up to two years. Stem cuttings offer better propagation results. Take cuttings in late spring or early summer.

REMARKS & ETYMOLOGY:
Carolus Linnaeus named it after the passion of Jesus Christ because it was long called *flor de las cinco llagas* (flower of the five wounds) by early Jesuit missionaries. They believed the various flower parts symbolized the crucifixion of Christ. The five sepals and five petals represented the ten faithful apostles, the fringe of filaments resembled the crown of thorns, the five stamens signifed the five wounds, and the three styles were the nails.

The blooms are spectaclar, especially the red-flowered tropical species. Passion flower was cultivated by the Native Americans in Virginia and has been used medicinally for such ailments as insomnia, sore eyes, and convulsions. The edible fruit makes nice jelly and sherbet. If you are trying to start *Passiflora* along rural fences you will need to keep livestock away; they love it.

SPECIES IN AMERICA:
About 500 species in American tropics.

REFERENCES:

Killip, E. P.
1938   The American species of Passifloraceae. *Publ. Field Mus. Nat. Hist., Bot. Ser.* 19:1–613.
Linnaeus, C.
1753   *Species Plantarum* 959.

PAVONIA
ROSE MALLOW

SCIENTIFIC NAME:
Pavonia lasiopetala Scheele 1848

FAMILY:
MALVACEAE

LIFE HISTORY:
Tender perennial shrub.

ORIGIN:
Southern North America.

RANGE:
Central Texas, and south to Mexico.

DESCRIPTION:
PLANT: Small shrub with many stems arising from base, up to 4′ tall and 3′ wide. Heart-shaped leaves.
FLOWER: Pink, hibiscus-like blossoms, 1″–2″ in diameter.

BLOOM PERIOD:
Intermittently from spring until fall.

POLLINATOR(S):
Bees.

HABITAT REQUIREMENTS:
Grows in shallow limestone soils, rocky woods, and the edges of thickets. Prefers full sun and well-drained soil.

PROPAGATION:
Collect seed as soon as capsule turns brown, but before it splits open. Seeds should be planted in the fall. Softwood cuttings can be taken in summer or fall.

REMARKS & ETYMOLOGY:
First discovered in Brazil, this plant's genus name honors Spanish botanist Jose Antonio Pavon (1754–1840), who collected extensively in South America. The species name, *lasiopetala* means "shaggy-petaled," and refers to the markedly hairy petals. Early Spanish explorers called pavonias *las rosas de San Juan*, or the roses of St. John. The honor of describing this *Pavonia* fell to a German botanist, Georg Heinrich Adolf Scheele (1808–1864).

The bark of the *Pavonia* species was a source of fibre for Native Americans. If you want to attract butterflies to your garden, this bright, pink flower is a must.

SPECIES IN AMERICA:
About 200 species, mostly tropical and subtropical.

REFERENCES:

Fryxell, P.
    1988   *Pavonia*, in Malvaceae of Mexico. *Syst. Bot. Monographs* 25:309–43.
Scheele, A.
    1848   *Linnaea* 21:470.

97

BEARD TONGUE
FOXGLOVE

SCIENTIFIC NAME:
Penstemon cobaea Nuttall 1837

FAMILY:
SCROPHULARIACEAE

LIFE HISTORY:
Perennial herb.

ORIGIN:
Central portions of the United States.

RANGE:
Nebraska to Texas.

DESCRIPTION:
PLANT: Erect, 1'–2' tall. Shiny leaves are coarsely toothed.
FLOWER: Flowers white, pale lavender or pink, streaked with purple lines.

BLOOM PERIOD:
April to June.

POLLINATOR(S):
Hummingbirds, bees.

HABITAT REQUIREMENTS:
Found in loam or rocky soils of prairies, bluffs and edges of creeks. Full sun.

PROPAGATION:
Foxglove grows easily from seed. If not available commercially, seed can be collected in the summer as soon as the capsules have dried. The seed often requires cold stratification before it will germinate. Plant in the fall, in well-drained soil.

REMARKS & ETYMOLOGY:
The botanical name for the genus is from the Latin, *paene* (almost, nearly), and the Greek, *stemon*, indicating that the staminode is almost a stamen. Thomas Nuttall (1786–1859), an early botanist in America, named the species because of its resemblance to species of the genus *Cobaea*. The fifth stamen is often covered with beard-like hairs, hence the common name "beard tongue."

The leaves of this eye-catching flower can be brewed into a laxative tea. It is certainly as worthy of cultivation as other member of the genus are. The seed capsules are hard and difficult to open—try the food processor using the sharp blade.

SPECIES IN AMERICA:
About 300 species in the Americas.

REFERENCES:

Crosswhite, F. S.
  1967   Revision of *Penstemon* section *Habroanthus* (Scrophulariaceae). *Amer. Midl. Naturalist* 77:1–41.
Nuttall, T.
  1837   *Proc. Amer. Phil. Soc.* n. s. 5:182.

BLUE CURLS

SCIENTIFIC NAME:
Phacelia congesta Hooker 1835

FAMILY:
HYDROPHYLLACEAE

LIFE HISTORY:
Annual or biennial herb.

ORIGIN:
Southwestern United States.

RANGE:
From the western half of Texas, to New Mexico, Colorado, Arizona, Utah, and Mexico.

DESCRIPTION:
PLANT: Erect, to 3′ tall, covered with soft, sticky hairs. Alternate leaves with irregularly toothed lobes.
FLOWER: Flowers blue or lavender, ¼″ diameter. Long, slender stamens with bright yellow anthers protrude conspicuously from flower.

BLOOM PERIOD:
March to June.

POLLINATOR(S):
Pollen- and nectar-collecting bees, scarab beetles, masarid wasps.

HABITAT REQUIREMENTS:
Found in sandy or rocky soils in prairies, woodland edges, and along stream banks. Full sun to dappled shade.

PROPAGATION:
Easily grown from seed, though not usually found commercially. Sow seed in well-drained soil.

REMARKS & ETYMOLOGY:
Yet another American plant described by W. J. Hooker, longtime director of the Royal Botanic Gardens in Kew, England. The genus name is derived from the Greek *phacelos,* meaning bundle, and refers to the clustered flowers. The species name, *congesta,* refers to the crowded arrangement of the buds.

There are eight or more tightly-coiled clusters of buds which unfurl as the flowers develop. *Phacelia congesta* often grows in large, showy colonies. Some species are cultivated as a crop to attract honey-producing bees.

SPECIES IN AMERICA:
About 200 species in the western United States and Mexico.

REFERENCES:

Atwood, N. D.
  1975   A revision of the *Phacelia crenulata* group for North America. *Great Basin Naturalist* 35:127–90.
Hooker, W. J.
  1835   *Bot. Mag.* 62: t. 3452.

DRUMMOND'S PHLOX

SCIENTIFIC NAME:
Phlox drummondii Hooker 1835

FAMILY:
POLEMONIACEAE

LIFE HISTORY:
Annual herb.

ORIGIN:
Central Texas.

RANGE:
Although native to central Texas, Drummond's phlox has become naturalized and cultivated throughout Texas and elsewhere. The species has several described subspecies or varieties.

DESCRIPTION:
PLANT: 6″–18″ tall; many stems arise from the base; may be prostrate.
FLOWER: Color varies from pink to white to lavender to red, and all shades between. Diameter of flower to one inch.

BLOOM PERIOD:
March to June.

POLLINATOR(S):
Moths, butterflies, hummingbirds.

HABITAT REQUIREMENTS:
Although phlox prefers fertile sandy soils, it also grows in well-drained alkaline soils. Sun to part shade.

PROPAGATION:
Seed is widely available commercially. Plant seed in the fall, at a recommended rate of ten pounds per acre. Allow plants to reseed for next year.

REMARKS & ETYMOLOGY:
The genus name is Greek for flame which refers to the vivid color of the flowers. The scientific name honors Thomas Drummond (1780–1835), a Scottish botanist who collected plants in Texas in the 1830s. It was named by William Jackson Hooker (1785–1865), a British botanist, director of the Royal Botanic Gardens, Kew, England, from 1842–1865.

Phlox has been bred extensively by European horticulturists and is now a colorful garden flower with many available cultivars. This species has been divided into six naturally occurring varieties that can be distinguished by their growth habit, flower color, and foliage.

SPECIES IN AMERICA:
About 50 species in temperate America.

REFERENCES:

Erbe, L. & B. L. Turner
    1962   A biosystematic study of the *Phlox cuspidata—Phlox drummondii* complex. *Amer. Midl. Naturalist* 67: 257–81.
Grant, V.
    1959   *Natural history of the phlox family*. The Hague: M. Nighoff.
Hooker, W. J.
    1835   *Bot. Mag.* 9: t. 3441.

FALSE DANDELION
TEXAS DANDELION

SCIENTIFIC NAME:
Pyrrhopappus pauciflorus de Candolle 1838

FAMILY:
ASTERACEAE (= COMPOSITAE)

LIFE HISTORY:
Annual herb.

ORIGIN:
North America.

RANGE:
Southwestern United States and Mexico.

DESCRIPTION:
PLANT: 6"–18" tall. Basal, oblanceolate, deeply lobed leaves about 3" long.
FLOWER: Flower heads yellow, 1"–2" diameter. Black to dark purple anther tubes occur in the center of each flower. Bisexual yellow ray flowers.

BLOOM PERIOD:
February to June.

POLLINATOR(S):
Butterflies, morning active specialist bees (restrict activities to particular species), other insects.

HABITAT REQUIREMENTS:
Grows in various dry soils of disturbed, open areas or prairies. Full sun.

PROPAGATION:
Like many composites, the seed of Texas dandelions have feathery tufts which aid in dispersal by wind. The numerous seeds germinate readily.

REMARKS & ETYMOLOGY:
Augustin Pyramaus de Candolle (1778–1841), a Swiss botanist, first described the species. Greek word for fire, *pyros,* and *pappos,* which refers to calyx-limb of composites, were combined to form the generic name. The specific name refers to the few-headed inflorescence (*pauci* = few; *florus* = flower).

The blooms of Texas dandelions, which last for several days, open facing the morning sun and follow it across the sky towards the west until they close at midday as the temperature increases. The young leaves can be boiled and eaten as greens. As with the common dandelion, it is a delight to blow the puffy heads and watch the plume-like seeds float with the breeze.

SPECIES IN AMERICA:
About three species in North America.

REFERENCES:

de Candolle, A. P.
1838   *Prodromus Systematis Naturalis Regni Vegetabilis,* 7:144.
Northington, D.
1974   Systematic studies of the genus *Pyrrhopappus* (Compositae, Cichorieae). *Spec. Publ. Mus. Texas Tech Univ.* 6:1–38.
Turner, B. L. and K.-J. Kim
1991   An overview of the genus *Pyrrhopappus* (Asteraceae: Lactuceae) with emphasis on chloroplast DNA restriction site data. *Amer. J. Bot.* 77:845–50.

MEXICAN HAT
PRAIRIE CONEFLOWER

SCIENTIFIC NAME:
Ratibida columnifera (Nuttall) 1813, Wooten & Standley 1813

FAMILY:
ASTERACEAE (= COMPOSITAE)

LIFE HISTORY:
Perennial herb.

ORIGIN:
North America.

RANGE:
Great Plains area of Midwest, west to Colorado and Wyoming and south to Mexico.

DESCRIPTION:
PLANT: Bushy, 1'–4' tall, with many branched stems.
FLOWER: Brown disk flowers project from a cylindrical green cone-like disk (1"–2" tall). Ray flowers, usually 4 to 10 per flower head, are variations of yellow and reddish-brown.

BLOOM PERIOD:
Summer to fall.

POLLINATOR(S):
Bees.

HABITAT REQUIREMENTS:
Prefers calcareous soils, but occurs in variety of soil types. Common in coastal areas and to altitudes above 7,000 feet. Full sun.

PROPAGATION:
Grows readily from seed and is widely available commercially. Seed can be collected in late summer. Fall planting is recommended, at a seeding rate of 2 to 4 pounds per acre.

REMARKS & ETYMOLOGY:
The common name "Mexican hat" was conferred because the tall disk made the flower resemble a Mexican sombrero to someone, but the meaning of *Ratibida* has not been determined. *Columnifera* refers to the markedly columnar receptacles which bear the tiny florets. Thomas Nuttall (1786–1859), an early naturalist, first described the species.

The blooms can last several days as cut flowers. When cultivated the species grows vigorously and is extremely drought tolerant. It often covers large areas of open prairies.

SPECIES IN AMERICA:
About six species in the eastern U.S.A. and Mexico.

REFERENCES:

Nuttall, T.
    1813   *Fraser's Catalogue No. 75.*
Richards, E. L.
    1968   A monograph of the genus *Ratibida. Rhodora* 70:348–93.
Wooten, E. & P. Standley
    1915   *Contr. U. S. Natl. Herb.* 19:706.

BLACK-EYED SUSAN

SCIENTIFIC NAME:
Rudbeckia hirta Linnaeus 1753

FAMILY:
ASTERACEAE (=COMPOSITAE)

LIFE HISTORY:
Annual or short-lived perennial herb.

ORIGIN:
United States.

RANGE:
Widespread throughout North America.

DESCRIPTION:
PLANT: 1'–3' tall. Stems and leaves covered with rough hairs.
FLOWER: Bisexual, reddish brown disk flowers surrounded by sterile, deep yellow ray flowers, 2"–3" in diameter.

BLOOM PERIOD:
April to September.

POLLINATORS:
Butterflies; solitary, specialist bees; soldier beetles, and nectar-feeding bee flies.

HABITAT REQUIREMENTS:
Prefers dry, acid soils of prairies, roadsides, and waste places. Full sun.

PROPAGATION:
Plant seed in spring or fall. Rake into loose topsoil. Recommended seeding rate is two to four pounds per acre. Wait until seed heads are quite dry and wear gloves while collecting.

REMARKS & ETYMOLOGY:
Named after Swedish professors Olaus J. Rudbeck (1630–1702), the father, and Olaus (1660–1740), the son, both botanists working prior to Carolus Linnaeus. The species name *hirta* means hairy or shaggy.

Uneaten by most livestock, Black-eyed Susan tends to become profuse on overgrazed land. Native Americans used juice from the roots to treat earaches, while the dried leaves and flowers were steeped and drunk as tonics. Although several quite different yellow flowers with dark centers are called Black-eyed Susans, this is the true one.

Transporting hay that included wildflower seed from the midwest to feed east coast livestock has spread this midwestern native to the Atlantic Coast where it now brightens the roadside. The domesticated Gloriosa Daisy, developed from *R. hirta,* makes a dramatic accent in the garden. Cut blossoms of both wild and domesticated Black-eyed Susans provide long lasting flower arrangements.

SPECIES IN AMERICA:
About 30 species in the temperate regions of North America.

REFERENCES:

Linnaeus, C.
1753   *Species Plantarum* 907.
Perdue, R. E., Jr.
1957   Synopsis of *Rudbeckia* subgenus *Rudbeckia. Rhodora* 59:293–99.

YELLOW TRUMPETS PITCHER PLANT

SCIENTIFIC NAME:
Sarracenia alata Wood 1863

FAMILY:
SARRACENIACEAE

LIFE HISTORY:
Perennial insectiverous herb.

ORIGIN:
Southern and eastern United States.

RANGE:
From the Gulf coastal plain of east Texas to southern Alabama.

DESCRIPTION:
PLANT: Stems 2'–3' tall. Forms clusters from rhizomes. Basal, yellow-green leaves are shaped into hollow, funnel-like tubes with terminal, red-veined hoods.
FLOWER: Nodding flowers face downwards, yellowish-green, often suffused with reddish-orange, about 2″ in diameter. Extraordinary, umbrella-like style.

BLOOM PERIOD:
March to June.

POLLINATOR(S):
Bees, perhaps flies.

HABITAT REQUIREMENTS:
Found in wet acid bogs and damp pinelands. Full sun to dappled shade.

PROPAGATION:
Seed can be collected in the fall, once the capsule has begun to split. Sow seed in pots indoors, and cold stratify for two months. The soil should be a low pH and high in moisture retention. Water plants from below. Keep plants in pots inside for the first year; transplant outside in the spring of the second year. Pitcher plants can also be propagated by root division.

REMARKS & ETYMOLOGY:
The genus name, *Sarracenia,* honors the seventeenth-century French botanist and physician Michael Sarrasin (1659–1734). *Alata,* the specific name, refers to the winged shape of the leaves. The author, Alphonso Wood (1810–1881), was an American botanist who published one of the first botany books in the United States (1845: *Class-Book of Botany*).

A nutrition-poor habitat has caused the pitcher plant to evolve an insectiverous lifestyle to increase its nutrition. Drawn by potent nectar, insects enter the leaf tubes. Once inside, they are trapped by soft hairs and then slide into the enzyme pool below, where they are digested. Pitcher plants are declining because drainage of bogs and swamps is causing loss of habitat. The curious form and habits of this unusual plant cause it to be overcollected. Most species are threatened or endangered. Many think the peculiar leaf is the bloom because the blooming period is so brief the flower is not often seen.

SPECIES IN AMERICA:
About 8 species in North America.

REFERENCES:

McDaniel, S.
1971   The genus *Sarracenia* (Sarraceniaceae). *Bull. Tall Timbers Res. Station* 9:15–17.
Wood, A.
1863   *Obj. Less. Bot.* 157.

SILVER LEAF NIGHTSHADE
TROMPILLO

SCIENTIFIC NAME:
Solanum elaeagnifolium Cavanilles 1795

FAMILY:
SOLANACEAE

LIFE HISTORY:
Perennial herb.

ORIGIN:
North America.

RANGE:
From Missouri and Kansas, south to Louisiana, Texas, Arizona and Mexico.

DESCRIPTION:
PLANT: Erect, spiny, many-branched, 1′–3′ tall. Leaves covered densely with tiny star-like hairs, producing a silvery sheen.
FLOWER: Light blue to purple flowers, 1″ in diameter, with prominent yellow anthers. Fruit is a yellow berry that turns black in summer and fall.

BLOOM PERIOD:
March to October.

POLLINATOR(S):
Bees.

HABITAT REQUIREMENTS:
Dry, disturbed soils of open woods, prairies and waste areas. Full sun.

PROPAGATION:
Noxious weed, not recommended for planting.

REMARKS & ETYMOLOGY:
This plant, first collected in Mexico, was described by a Spanish clergyman and botanist Antonio José Cavanilles (1745–1804), who was director of the botanical gardens in Madrid, Spain. *Solanum* is the classical Latin name for a plant. The specific name means "with leaves like species of the genus *Elaeagnus*."

Ripe berries can be toxic to animals, including humans. Even small amounts can cause severe poisoning or death. Despite their harmful constituents, the berries have many practical applications. Navajo Indians used the berries to curdle milk in cheese making, while the Kiowas mixed the fruit with brain tissue to tan buck skins. Other Native Americans used Trompillo for the treatment of ailments such as toothaches and sore throats.

SPECIES IN AMERICA:
Genus of over 1,700 species, mostly tropical, in both North and South America.

REFERENCES:

Cavanilles, A. J.
    1795   *Icones et descriptiones planatarum* 3:22, t. 243.
Heiser, C. W., Jr.
    1969   *Nightshades: The paradoxical plants.* San Francisco: W. H. Freeman & Co.
Mohlenbrock, R. H.
    1990   *Nightshades to mistletoe.* Carbondale: Southern Illinois University Press.

GREENTHREAD

SCIENTIFIC NAME:
Thelesperma filifolium (Hooker) 1836, Gray 1884

FAMILY:
ASTERACEAE (= COMPOSITAE)

LIFE HISTORY:
Annual or weak perennial herb.

ORIGIN:
North America.

RANGE:
From Louisiana north to Missouri, Arkansas, Kansas, and Nebraska, and west to Texas, Oklahoma, New Mexico and Colorado.

DESCRIPTION:
PLANT: Bushy, few to many-branched, 1″–3″ tall. Leaves are divided into many linear segments.
FLOWER: Flower heads 1″–2″ diameter. Usually 8 yellow ray flowers and many yellow or reddish-brown disk flowers.

BLOOM PERIOD:
Late spring to summer or early fall.

POLLINATOR(S):
Butterflies, bees, other insects.

HABITAT REQUIREMENTS:
Found in dry soils of prairies, disturbed areas, and roadsides. Full to partial shade.

PROPAGATION:
Seed is not widely available commercially, but can be hand-collected. Collect seeds as soon as they are ripe (summer or fall). Store in a cool, well-ventilated place. Sow seed in the fall in a well-drained area with plenty of sun.

REMARKS & ETYMOLOGY:
The newly found wildflower seed received by William J. Hooker, Director of the Royal Botanic Gardens in Kew, England, during 1834, were collected in Texas by Thomas Drummond. The translated specific name, *filifolium,* or "little thread," refers to the thread-like leaves, while the genus is called *thele* or nipple-seed on account of the nipple-like pappus units on the seed or fruit (dry, indehiscent achene).

Thelesperma is frequently confused with *Coreopsis.* The threadlike leaves of *Thelesperma* make it quite drought-tolerant.

SPECIES IN AMERICA:
About 12 species occur in the central and western United States and Mexico.

REFERENCES:

Gray, A.
    1849   *Hooker's J. Bot. Kew Gard. Misc.* 1:252.
Hooker, W. J.
    1836   *Bot. Mag.* t. 3505.
Shinners, L. H.
    1950   The Texas species of *Thelesperma. Field & Lab.* 18:17–18.

GIANT SPIDERWORT
WIDOW'S TEARS

SCIENTIFIC NAME:
Tradescantia gigantea Rose 1899

FAMILY:
COMMELINACEAE

LIFE HISTORY:
Perennial herb.

ORIGIN:
North America.

RANGE:
Endemic to central Texas.

DESCRIPTION:
PLANT: Erect plant, 1'–3' tall. Linear leaves 4"–12" long. The upper stems covered with short hairs.
FLOWER: Lavender, blue or pink flowers, about 1" in diameter.

BLOOM PERIOD:
March to May.

POLLINATOR(S):
Pollen-collecting bees since flowers lack nectar.

HABITAT REQUIREMENTS:
Moist limestone soils of pastures, edges of woods and roadsides. Shade to part sun.

PROPAGATION:
Easily propagated from seed or transplanted. The thin tuberous roots should be planted immediately. Once established they multiply readily.

REMARKS & ETYMOLOGY:
The genus name honors John Tradescant (1608–1662), a Hollander who came to England before 1620 as gardener to King Charles the First. He was noted for his introductions of exotic plants. His son visited Virginia, returning with several new plants, among them *Tradescantia*. The species name *gigantea* refers to the large size. The common name, spiderwort, alludes to the jointed stems which resemble a spider's leg. Joseph Nelson Rose (1862–1928), an American botanist, first described it.

Instead of persisting for some time as in most flowers, the petals of *Tradescantia* are reportedly dissolved rather rapidly by enzyme secretions and soon deliquesce, hence the name "widow's tears." Cell mutations in the petals of Spiderworts have been found to be susceptible to mutation when exposed to environmental pollution and radiation. Because of this they have been used as monitors for such detection.

SPECIES IN AMERICA:
About 60 species in temperate and tropical America.

REFERENCES:

Anderson, E. & R. W. Woodson
    1935   The species of *Tradescantia* indigenous to the United States. *Contr. Arnold Arbor.* 9:73–74.
Rose, J. N.
    1899   *Contr. U.S. Natl. Herb.* 5:205.

WAKE ROBIN
COAST TRILLIUM

SCIENTIFIC NAME:
Trillium ovatum Pursh 1814

FAMILY:
LILIACEAE

LIFE HISTORY:
Perennial herb.

ORIGIN:
Western and northern America.

RANGE:
From Montana to British Columbia, south to Colorado and California.

DESCRIPTION:
PLANT: Stems 9″–16″ tall. Three broad, ovate leaves.
FLOWER: White flowers, 1″–2″ in diameter, these gradually turn deep pink with age.

BLOOM PERIOD:
Late March to June.

POLLINATOR(S):
Beetles and flies.

HABITAT REQUIREMENTS:
Found in moist woods or bogs, up to 7000′ elevation. Full or dappled shade.

PROPAGATION:
Species of *Trillium* are difficult to propagate because the seed have high dormancy and a slow growth rate. As many as six or more years may be necessary for *trillium* to reach flowering stage. In nature the seed are dispersed by ants. Most plants in nurseries are from rhizomes that have been collected from the wild because they are so difficult to propagate from seed. The result is a population decline in the wild. Many species of *Trillium* are listed as threatened or endangered.

REMARKS & ETYMOLOGY:
The genus name, *Trillium*, is in reference to the flower and leaf parts being in threes. The species name, *ovatum*, means ovate, referring to the shape of the leaves. When Frederick Traugott Pursh (1774–1820), a German botanical traveler, described *T. ovatum*, the state of Oregon, where this species is now so loved, was a very sparsely populated, distant land.

The flowering of Wake Robins initiates the beginning of spring. Native Americans used the root to ease the pain of childbirth, calling it birthroot. The flowers remain open for about two weeks, gradually changing color from white to rose all the while. Not all species of *Trillium* have blooms as spectacular as those of *T. ovatum*.

SPECIES IN AMERICA:
About 25 species in temperate North America.

REFERENCES:

Gates, R. R.
1917   A systematic study of the North American *Trillium*, its variabalility, and its relation to *Paris medeola. Ann. Missouri Bot. Gard.* 4:59–61.
Pursh, F. T.
1814   *Flora Americae Septentrionalis* 1:245.

PRAIRIE VERBENA
DAKOTA VERVAIN

SCIENTIFIC NAME:
Verbena bipinnatifida Nuttall 1821

FAMILY:
VERBENACEAE

LIFE HISTORY:
Perennial herb.

ORIGIN:
North central regions of the United States.

RANGE:
From South Dakota to Missouri and Alabama, west to Texas, Colorado, New Mexico and Arizona.

DESCRIPTION:
PLANT: Low-growing, 4″–12″ tall. Leaves with narrow incised lobes.
FLOWER: Lavender or pink five-lobed flowers (about ⅜″ long) in rounded, terminal clusters.

BLOOM PERIOD:
Spring to fall.

POLLINATOR(S):
Butterflies, bees, and other insects.

HABITAT REQUIREMENTS:
Found in dry sandy or calcareous plains, prairies, slopes and roadsides. Full sun.

PROPAGATION:
Can be propagated by seed, cuttings or transplants. Available commercially. Numerous form and color varieties have been developed.

REMARKS & ETYMOLOGY:
Thomas Nuttall (1786–1859), an early botanist and naturalist in America, placed this species in the genus *Verbena*, which is the Latin name for any ceremonial or medicinal plant; however, its actual application in this instance is obscure. The species name describes the bipinnate leaves which were used for ceremonial or medicinal purposes by early man.

 Verbena contains tannins and verbenalin, both effective in tonics for reducing fevers. The flowers are especially rich in butterfly-attracting nectar.

 Recent workers (Umber, 1979) have recognized *Verbena bipinnatifida* and related species as belonging to the genus *Glandularia*, first proposed by Nuttall himself in 1837.

SPECIES IN AMERICA:
Over 200 species in temperate and tropical America.

REFERENCES:

Nuttall, T.
  1821   *J. Acad. Nat. Sci. Philadelphia.* 2:123.
Perry, L. M.
  1933   A revision of the North American species of *Verbena. Ann. Missouri Bot. Gard.* 20:323–25.
Umber, R. E.
  1979   The genus *Glandularia* (Verbenaceae) in North America. *Syst. Bot.* 4:72–102.

INDEX TO
THE WILDFLOWERS

AMERICAN WILDFLOWER FLORILEGIUM

Art Direction, typographic design
and layout were by Caissa Douwes.

The typeface for this book is Bembo.
The type was set by G&S Typesetters.

Plates 18, 20, 27, and 52 were made using especially commissioned
photography by Christopher Zaleski, Zaleski Studio. All other
plates were separated directly from Jean Andrews' original
gouache and color-pencil drawings.

American Wildflower Florilegium was printed and bound by
Nissha Printing Company, Kyoto, Japan. The plates were made from
175-line screen separations and printed in four-color offset
lithography on 157 gsm Mitsubishi New V Matte.